EON

EVOLUTION AND
OPINIONS OF A NEWJACK

KIP LEE

AFRAMEDIA PRESS INC.

LIBRARY OF CONGRESS CARD CATALOG NUMBER: 95-081185

ISBN 0-9649734-0-5

FORWARD

I dedicate this book to my grandmother who took the time to raise me and protect me to adulthood. To this day, I do not know where your strength and faith came from. I hope to be worthy of your efforts.

To my father, I thank you for being in the house and being married to my mother. I thank you for showing me how men get up each and every morning and go to work. And have no fear, Kipco will never be a bum. Rest in Peace Both of You.

To my mother for putting up with my mess, diapers included, for my entire life.

ACKNOWLEDGMENTS

Much thanx to Marie for editing the confusion I handed to her and making some sense of it. Thanx to Jeff for his candid, frank criticism and for bringing much comedy to my life over many years. Nuff luv yawl.

TABLE OF CONTENTS

INTRODUCTION... 1

ON WHITE: NATURE OF THE COLLECTIVE CONSCIOUSNESS........ 5

COLLECTIVE PERSONA 8
ZERO SUM SCARCITY MENTALITY 12
PARANOIA 13
NATURE OF THEIR SICKNESS 15
IDENTITY CRISIS 19
BURDEN OF LEGITIMIZATION... 20
DENIAL... 24
INSECURITY AND FEAR 27
ARROGANCE OF IGNORANCE 28
WHEN THE ILLUSION FAILS... 35
TACTICS: POKE MY EYES OUT AND CONDEMN ME FOR BEING BLIND 38
ENVIRONMENT 40
THE WHITE COLLECTIVE VS. THE PAST 45
SOCIALIZED TIGHT ASSES 49
EMBODIMENT 51
CONCLUSION 53
DERAILMENT 59

ON BLACK 60

HISTORY... 62
PROBLEMS FACED TODAY 64
WE LACK SELF CONCEPT AND VISION TO APPROACH THE FUTURE 67
BUT WE'RE VICTIMS! 72
ARE WE TO BLAME?.. 72
    Assimilation... 73
    Cycles of Awareness... 78
    To Damn Competitive and Elitist... 80
    Reinforce White Supremacy... 84
    Maintenance of the Slave Relationship... 86
    Assuming Their Standards 89
    They Will Realize The Error of Their Ways 91
BLACK MEN 91
    Quest for Manhood 93
    I Just Wanna Be a Nigga.. 96
    A Basic Level of Self Hate, Rage and Mistrust............................... 97

WOMEN 99
    Self Esteem/Hate and Assertion *102*
    Are Men to Blame? *104*
    Are Women to Blame? *105*
    What They Really Want *106*
OUR CHILDREN 106
OUR MUSIC 109
CHURCH 110
THE ANSWER 114
    Don't Make Excuses for Greatness *114*
    The Other Man *116*
    Education *117*
    Cut the BS and Get Up Off It! *118*
    Destruction of Our Leaders *119*
    We Have Not Leveraged Ourselves to Implement Change *120*
    Ultimate Responsibility *121*

ON AMERICA **122**

CORPORATE AMERIKKKA 124
IT'S THEIR FRAT 126
THE GOVERNMENT 128
THE AMERICAN WAY 131
THE LEGACY OF "OUR" FATHERS 134
EVENTS OF LATE 137
    The Gulf War *137*
    Rodney King *140*
    OJ *141*
    The Million Man March *142*
ENVIRONMENT 143
THE FLIP SIDE 147
FOREIGN RELATIONS 149
MONEY 151
    Justice *154*
    Education *155*
    Health *156*
    Two Sides of a Coin *156*
    Tool of the Disenfranchised *157*
    Dividends of the Environment *158*
A NARROW PERSPECTIVE 158
WHAT AMERICA MUST DO 159

ON NEWJACK **162**

WHERE WE COME FROM 163
OUR RESPONSIBILITY 164
THE ENVIRONMENT 166
ATTITUDE 169
NEWJACKISIMS 169

APPENDIX **176**

20 TACTICS OF OPPRESSION 176

INTRODUCTION

I'm a single, twenty something, black male, born and raised in the United States of America. My earliest childhood memories were of the Civil Rights Movement, the assassinations of Malcolm X and Reverend Dr. Martin Luther King, the Vietnam War, Henry Aaron hitting number 715, and the original Jackson Five. I do not come from a dysfunctional family nor a single parent home. I was not raised in the inner city. I was raised in the suburbs. I have lived my entire life in a white neighborhood and received my education in the white public school system. I have never been in trouble with the law and have never once experimented with illegal drugs. Sometimes when I wonder whether I'm truly a black man, something happens every day to remind me that indeed I am. Due to the diligent efforts and sacrifice of my family, to whom I am forever indebted, I am here regardless of statistical profiles and stereotypes that describe who I should be. I am college educated and currently hold a job in corporate America. I have a condo, several vehicles, an active social live, a supportive family, and the best set of friends that anyone could wish for. The state in which I exist is not only exceptional for a black man in America, it is exceptional for any man anywhere on this earth. I recognize that I am truly blessed. I also realize that I live a fairy tale. My friends and family will probably be shocked when they read the material that is about to be communicated. Its candor, its bleeding edge frankness is more indicative of someone that had it a little tougher coming up.

As a black person, I believe that there is a price for living a comfortable life when you do not possess the true freedom of being self sufficient. When someone else other than yourself signs your paycheck (pay for staying in check), someone that may have no real concern for you as a human being, someone that may not even think you to be a human being. You are forced to endure the lies and the illusions of a mainstream society in a repressive state of denial. You are involuntarily forced to tolerate the people that perpetuate these lies in order to provide yourself with employment. You become infuriated with their arrogance and ignorance. These people believe that the rest of us are stupid enough to listen to the words that come forth from their mouths, while ignoring their actions that are contrary to all they say. It is ultimately insulting to see the attempts aimed at dismissing the black community being perpetrated before our eyes every day. This while we "privileged" members of the community are provided incentives to distance ourselves from our brothers and sisters and become part of the mainstream. It is also frustrating that our community is not hip enough to the game to provide for its own well being and take charge of its own destiny by cutting all ties related to our dependency. Perhaps living in this comfortable state of hypocrisy is what's gotten to me as of late, and the reason I unexpectedly became a writer.

I began writing this book five years ago after having just graduated from the engineering school of one of the prestigious historically black universities in 1990, and securing a job as an engineer in corporate America. I moved away from my friends to be closer to work and concentrated on starting my career on the right foot. Starting my first real job was challenging but I adjusted to deadlines, budgets, and company politics without problems. However, something happened to me that first year out of school. Something that ended my fairy tale sheltered existence. It was as if someone had lifted the flood gates on my repressed consciousness and all this stuff came pouring out uncontrollably and without warning. My mind became a freight train and I was the one in its path. I had trouble keeping up with my own thoughts. I was forced to buy a pocket tape recorder because I found myself scribbling on every piece of paper within reach. I would scribble in meetings, during lunch, and driving home in the evening. I had an almost adversarial relationship with my own mind. It began to interfere with my work and I suffered from insomnia. For a short while I found myself taking sleeping pills for the first time in my life. Three years later after having purchased a computer and organizing the many scribbled pages and tape recordings of the thoughts that traveled my mind, I found myself completing this short book. This book is the assembly of a three-year mental odyssey that has challenged my mind and made me question the conditions surrounding our society. It is a milestone in the journey that I take toward enlightenment and self awareness. It is my initial therapeutic release of what I hold inside every day. I am proud to share it with you.

What follows are my uncensored, raw, opinions on a variety of topics dealing with our societies current state of existence from a black perspective. It is not my intention to candy-coat my opinions in any manner. Candy-coating issues is not something that I practice nor care to do. I will not engage in political double talk since I have no constituents to whom I must answer, and I had complete freedom in writing this book. I answered only to God. Some of the opinions that I mention will be offensive to people who do not see things as I do, or who realize that I have exposed them for who they truly are. My greatest wish is to strike some nerve in everyone that reads this material and deny people the ability to ignore it.

Many who read this work may be confronted with their true selves for the first time. I am willing to risk my comfortable lifestyle on the opinions that I have expressed since that is what men do. No level of comfort that I have attained thus far is worth holding back my opinions or dulling their edge. I, in particular, gear this book toward my people who are searching for something, who are frustrated, who are confused, who want hard-core uncensored, unfiltered, nonpolitical, information on how the big picture is put together. I do not profess to have all or even a small majority of the answers to the questions plaguing our community. I will discuss in great candor my opinions on white people, black people, men, women, America, and every topic in between that I feel relevant to our lives. Most importantly, I will discuss the attitude that I feel that our people need to adopt in order to deal with life. It's an uncompromising Newjack attitude. I will try to offer as many answers as I can. This is not a complaint book. This book is not for the faint hearted or those in a state of denial who want to continue to digest lies that make them happy or comfortable. This book is my therapy and I hope that at least one thing that I say is different from anything you have ever heard before.

On White: Nature of the Collective Consciousness

I begin with the topic that will be the most controversial and receive the most attention. Some people will not get past the first few pages due to discomfort or denial. This is not my problem since I must remain true to my message. Why is it that I feel I'm qualified to speak on white people? Perhaps because except for four years of my life (college), they were who I went to school with, lived with, worked with, and to some extent socialized with. Though all my closest friends at this time are all black, I believe that a part of me exists within the white collective mind set. I understand where they are coming from as well as where they need to go. These people have been demystified due to my continuous exposure to them. Part of our problem as black people with regard to white people is simply that we do not know who they are, nor understand their actions and attitudes. As for myself, I fight a daily battle to separate my self concept from that of white people by not measuring myself by white standards. Much of what they do is poisonous and foreign to our community. They flood us with imagery and impose consequences that are not in our best interests. I do maintain white friendships and get along well with those whites that respect me. For my white friends with whom I share this work, I make no apologies nor experience any regrets. I speak on the collective mind set of a majority of white people not just a few select decent individuals that I have had the opportunity to know.

From a black perspective, white people are a relevant topic of discussion due to the crossing of our histories. There is the presence of one consistent element in every explanation that attempts to address the present sorry state of affairs that the world has been forced to endure for the last 400 years. This element takes the form of one group of individuals who instigate, orchestrate, and perpetuate the conditions that are the source of unrest and disorder in the world today. All for the express written purpose of affording themselves advantage and oppressing others. This group is responsible for every major war that has taken place and the conditions that have brought the world to the brink of destruction on more than one occasion. This group is responsible for the institutionalism of slavery, the murder of millions of people of color, the bastardization and rape of the black race, hate groups, racism, the beating of Rodney King, Watergate, Iran contra, BCCI, the drug trade, organized crime, the S&L crisis, insider trading, world pollution, global warming, the near extinction of thousands of species and entire civilizations, and millions of other atrocities that have, as yet, gone undiscovered. Ironically, this group still has control of the reins of society due to their ability to force others to abide by their dictates. They are the worlds original barbarians and bullies. Naturally I am referring to the collective of white people. More specifically, white males. Even more specifically the white male consciousness that is the most pervasive, warped, and influential element in our society. One cannot exist without being impacted in some form by the oppressive characteristics of this university of thought. This mindset manifests itself through political policy, financial institutions, and overt racism, all of which are related. When I refer to whites, or to white people, or to the white man in this text, I am not referring to an individual or even an actual physical group of people. I am referring to the white male consciousness that is indicative of the attitudes and actions of some segments of their race. I refer to the consciousness that some white people tap into in varying degrees, and I will comment on the most severe and extreme degree of alignment with this consciousness. I also naturally realize that not all whites make a career out of doing black people harm. Some of the good intentioned ones even happen to be white males. Anything that I say will not offend well-intentioned whites since they will understand my mistrust and anger if indeed they are genuine and sincere in their actions. For those whites that are not of conscience or those that straddle the fence of consciousness, I hope to sincerely offend and shake the sandy foundation upon which you stand and by which you define yourself. Not that I expect you to change, however I do intend to bring you out into the light and take the sheet off for all to view.

If there were objective observers of humanity, they would be forced to ask the question, "How did a minority on the planet become the collective controlling body of the planet?" The answer to this question lies in the nature of the creature, as well as its established history of interaction with the other inhabitants of the planet. A study of this subject would reveal a people and history prone toward barbarism, deception, rape and conquest for monetary profit that translates into power, which translates into control. The goal of this controlling body of white society is complete domination of their environment. Whites operate on one very simple principle, **FEAR**. The fear of disappearing and losing an identity based on the color of their skin, or lack there of. The farther away one is from being white, the larger the threat posed to white people. This is based on the fact that only someone that is nonwhite can remove a white person's whiteness which is the core of their identity. Sentiments to this effect have been uttered by people such as Dr. Frances Cress Welsing who has described the fear of white genetic annihilation. Material of this nature is of great interest and should be read, however it is not a requirement since every person is qualified to be

a genetic engineer. If you are unsure of your qualifications allow me
to describe the only required knowledge in the form of the applicable
equations. They are as follows:

Black Man + White Woman = Black baby
White Man + Black Woman = Black Baby
Black Man + Black Woman = Black Baby
White Man + White Woman = White Baby

The last equation is the only one that provides for white survival.
A society where whites are not physically distinctive as being white,
is the worst fear of the white man because they will have lost
everything that they believe makes them superior. Understand one
simple concept. ***The basis for the actions of whites is the threat of
losing their whiteness and all the advantages that it affords.*** Fear
would be the natural reaction if you were aware that someone
outside of your race had the power to genetically alter your very
identity and appearance. A being of such power would have to be
subdued and rendered powerless. Whites are ultimately afraid of the
being who is physically and spiritually completely opposite from
themselves. Naturally, this is the **BLACK MALE**. I mention the
black male because only a black male can impregnate a white female
and have a black child, thus removing whiteness. Whites fear of this
prospect is evident in their paranoid behavior and violent actions
against black men such as Emmit Till. Others like him also suffer
due to the threat of a black man in sexual union with a white female.
From a white perspective all factors that could potentially bring this
scenario to light must be eliminated.

Collective Persona

The collective conciseness of whites is a fascinating one. It basses
itself on an extremely arrogant view of being superior by nature with

the divine right to rule all who are nonwhite. Naturally this inflated self concept is a falsehood, and deep down whites do realize it. They expend considerable effort in covering up this reality. If it were generally known that white's ability to destroy, murder, steal, and change history was the source of their power, they would never be able to maintain the choke hold they have on today's society. Therefore, they are forced to legitimize their presence and stature with glitz, public relations, illusion, propaganda and complete fabrication. If you tell yourself a lie enough times, you will begin to believe it. Whites have fallen victim to their own self-proclaimed greatness, and it has only served to perpetuate the arrogance of these people all compounded by the fact that so many others have bought into their lies. It has led to an over abundance of the narrow white male viewpoint that has, in general, lead to the degradation of the quality of life for everyone else.

Whites' twisted love of self is almost admirable from a positive self image perspective. In the eyes of whites, whites can do no wrong. They celebrate their criminals in the movies and books. White politicians are almost untouchable regardless of the nature of their crimes. History has made heroes out of barbarians such as Columbus and Napoleon. White support mechanisms function effectively largely due to the fact that whites have total control of the media and entertainment. Their control of these institutions and their distorted view of self has affected other cultures exposed to this media campaign. Blacks in particular are taught to hate their appearance, that white is good and black is bad, and that blond hair and blue eyes are the standard of beauty. Many weak souls fall into this trap where whites have taken advantage of the ability to program the human mind by instilling the images they have chosen.

Whites symbolize their collective being as a sterile clean room where all foreign nonwhite objects are considered contaminants. This pure atmosphere is extremely sensitive to all impurities or nonwhites. It is the duty of all members of this elite society to continually monitor the conditions of their environment to maintain the present atmosphere and defend against outside elements. The people in this atmosphere have little incentive to explore or understand that which lies outside its confines since defending the clean room is a burdensome task. As a result whites have little regard for the members of other cultures and have no desire to learn anything about others. All that lies outside the clean room is dubbed as inferior and is considered fair game for exploitation and consumption.

Within the confines of the clean room, there is a social hierarchy and order of operation. Whites are basically fragmented into three levels based on education and economics. Those with the most money, education, and social upbringing, are the **upper-level whites** who have the highest level of control and power. These individuals are the ones that implement the policies that we all live by. The **mid-level whites** are those that strive hardest to be in the upper-level. It is actually these whites who cause the most disturbance in society because they experience the frustration of not being in the upper-level. These whites must improve their condition at the expense of someone else, and must maintain their condition by keeping others in a downtrodden position. The **lower-level whites** are those that are poor and uneducated who no one really cares about. This group is frustrated because they realize that they will never be in the upper social structure of their own people. They also find it necessary to have someone to look down on from another race to determine that they have some value. The lowest and highest categories of whites are similar with regard to their level of ignorance. The highest category of whites is ignorant due to the fact that they have the money to physically separate themselves from everyone else. They simply don't have a lot of interaction with those outside their social standing. Lower-level whites are ignorant because they are just naturally stupid and feel the need to blame others for their sorry state. The most play and interaction occur between the mid- and upper-level whites since the former seeks admittance into the latter. Between these two layers, upper-level whites pledge the mid-level whites into their fraternity. After the mid-level whites have gained admittance, they completely deny their origins and vehemently maintain that they have been upper-level whites for their entire lives. Upper-level and mid-level whites do not particularly give a damn about lower-level whites except under certain circumstances. The lower-level whites are largely the ones that join the overt white supremacist groups. Upper-level and mid-level whites cannot afford to join such groups since they must maintain a certain illusionist anonymous demeanor. Even though they will secretly support the emotions and sentiments uttered by the supremacist groups. The mid- and upper-levels will also secretly funnel funding to these groups. This support is due to the fact that the upper- and mid-level whites will utilize the lower-level whites to carry out the radical actions that they in their heart support, yet cannot afford to be implicated. The lower-level whites serve to divert attention away from the actions of the mid- and upper-level whites. They also comprise the occupational fighting force of the white race that will carry out the actions that the mid- and upper-levels are afraid to carry out for fear of bloodying themselves. Due to the need for this type of fighting function, the higher layers have no intention of improving the condition of lower-level whites. Thus there is yet another sub-division amongst whites between the covert illusionist upper- and mid-level whites and overt exaggerated lower-level whites. Lower-level whites count on the distant support of the higher layers since they are too uneducated and ignorant to support themselves. It all works out pretty well. When I refer to the white consciousness, I refer mainly to the consciousness shared by the mid- and upper-levels. The lower-level whites think that they are superior because the higher levels believe they are superior and all are associated by race. The lower-level is too dumb to put even flawed reasoning behind their fallacy of supremacy.

Beyond the measure of economics and education it is possible to further describe whites in the more general terms of human decency. All three economic groups can be further divided by this measure of decency. The breakdown is as follows:

- **25%** of whites are generally of good nature and decent. These whites are self aware, secure individuals that intend no one any harm and are supportive of all people regardless of color. It is my pleasure to have some of them as my friends.
- **50%** of whites are those that straddle the fence of decency, oriented slightly toward the indecent. These are the whites that oscillate between decent behavior when the camera is on and attention is upon them, and indecent behavior when implementing their agenda, or when they know they can get away with it. Just like the mid-level economic whites, this group is the most dangerous due to their two-faced tendency to backstab if the opportunity presents itself.
- The remaining **25%** of whites are those that are simply indecent. These folks are ignorant, self centered, insecure and base their value upon holding back and looking down at nonwhites. They bring no value to society whatsoever.

Zero Sum Scarcity Mentality

Whites have a scarcity mentality. They believe that there are simply limited resources that must be secured exclusively for whites. They view the advancement of entire peoples in this manner. Whites believe that advancement for an individual or a group of nonwhite people must logically mean a step back for white people. This is the reason that some whites will act to hold back the advancement of nonwhites for no apparent reason. They scream about affirmative action and quotas because they feel as though they are being denied opportunity. They believe that there are but so many jobs, so much money, so many fine homes, and but so much that is acceptable for nonwhites to possess. They impose the burden upon themselves to decide what nonwhites should have and just how much.

Paranoia

Whites walk through life like it is a mine field. They are leery of their environment to the extent that they must have an ear to the ground at all times to avoid their naturally paranoid condition from taking over. Whites are well aware of what it is they are up against. Even during slavery, the white masters found it necessary to outlaw the slaves to read. They feared the slaves would gain knowledge and be better able to communicate to expose white lies and illusion, in order to liberate themselves from their oppressed condition. Why would anyone who claims to be superior be fearful of someone reading if they were not in an insecure state? Whites know that they are not superior and realize that any other people can achieve what they have done if left alone, unhindered. Whites simply don't want other people to realize their potential and become stiff competition in environments that whites have created exclusively for whites to dominate. If other people show the ability to perform on par with whites, the illusion of white superiority is ruined. As a result the white position of authority is compromised.

Ironically, whites are paranoid to the extent that they are fearful of one another at the upper levels of the power structure and as a result exhibit their naturally cannibalistic tendencies. Few white European countries can meet eye to eye on any given subject except for their mutual agreement to rape Africa collectively and if necessary argue over the spoils. The Berlin Wall just fell, Yugoslavia is torn by factional fighting, and many European countries are still in a barbarous state with regard to how its people are treated and their living conditions. It wasn't long ago that the two biggest white kids on the block were fearful of squaring off against one another. It just so happens that communism failed due to economic conditions and democracy won out by default. No one knows better than whites what whites are capable of. Notice how whites feel the strict need to clearly separate their territory from that of other whites to avoid potential confrontations. Whites must lay

13

everything out in such explicit detail that there is no room for ambiguity. Look at their contracts and documents that lay out agreements amongst themselves. They will seek advantage over one another, but there is a camaraderie and sick admiration for the white guy that can ramrod the other white guy to his advantage.

White fear emanates in its purist form at the physical level. As was previously stated, whites have an intense fear of genetic annihilation to the extent that they are even more comfortable around light skinned blacks than darker. Whites consider lighter skin tone less of a threat. The sexual presence of black males as well as the physical presence of black males has always frightened whites. Former President Bush used a simple campaign add to get elected. He used Willie T. Horton as a powerful image to amplify the already paranoid nature of whites by allowing them to imagine their daughters being raped by this rough looking black man and becoming impregnated with a black child. The add worked. White males secretly have a natural inferiority complex when they compare themselves physically to black males, and as a result act many times out of jealous rage toward black men.

Whites are most comfortable around blacks who are not threatening and wagging our tails, as it were, and buck dancing. They like us when we are serving them, when we are entertaining them, and in particular when we are acting like buffoons and making them laugh; an *Amos and Andy Syndrome*. Whites express extreme sensitivity at the first mention or hint that blacks may take any form of action, especially violent action. This country seems to pay particular attention to any mention of taking action against white folks or their institutions. Rapper Ice T's Cop Killer song sent this country into a paranoid tail spin not long ago. I guess this is our legacy left from Ole Nat Turner. God bless his courageous soul.

The greatest fear of the white man is that there will be no distinctive white people afforded advantage. He fears at the end of the game the white man will not have all the marbles or any large portion there of, in his possession. Whites fear that the truth about them and their lack of original culture, history, and evolution will be discovered. They fight at every turn of the corner to keep the self-praising PR campaign firmly in place to avoid this eventuality.

Nature of Their Sickness

How could any people commit the most brutal and savage crimes throughout history, down play or blatantly deny them, and continue to perpetrate the same actions? More specifically, the sickest consciousness that humanity has ever produced is that of the white male. The demeanor of this creature is like that of a rabid, white, pit-bull terrier pushed into a corner and forced to fight. The deception and duplicity of this animal lie in its ability to transform itself at will into the guise of a lap dog yet maintain it's naturally vicious nature. White males do not have the ability to associate themselves with the problems they have created. This results in a refusal to assume responsibility for their past evil actions. They go to great lengths to portray their campaign of propaganda and onslaught against black men. They depict men such as Emmitt Till, Yusef Hawkins, Rodney King and a million others, as a societal problem or social short-coming manifesting itself. People are even afraid to point to white males as the source of these problems, since they command a certain degree of power and influence. People are scared and dance around the issue to avoid pointing a finger directly at white males. However, I would like to officially identify white males as the poison pill of our society. There is no other group that has been consistently responsible for social unrest and disorder on a global scale. It would almost seem as though the consistent behavior of some white males is part of a coordinated effort to denigrate nonwhites. However these people are not so smart that they have crafted some grand conspiracy with vision toward the future. They merely have what every dog is born with by nature, a drive to survive and a desire to screw everything that they come across.

EON

The inferiority complex of the white male is what he hides in the guise of superiority. The white male is ultimately frustrated at his inability to express himself through the raw physicality of his own body in the manner that nonwhite males do. However, to the extent that he has psyched himself out and been physically eliminated, the white male cannot assert himself in the most colorful of fashions (i.e., popular sports). Therefore the white male has assumed other venues of assertion where he can act as the master or boss. The equivalent of the white male's Michael Jordan is the figure of Gordon Gekko played by Michael Douglas in the movie Wall Street. The white mans slam dunk is equivalent to his manipulation of economics for monetary profit. The white mans home run is his manipulation of people to assert his power and further his interests. The white man gets as much joy in sending a fax and participating in a conference call or power lunch, as others get in strenuous physical activity.

It is simple to see where white behavior comes from, by placing yourself in their historical shoes and imagining the environment in which they developed. Picture yourself existing in a state of developmental dormancy, while the rest of the world passes you by in every aspect. You've had to deal with an ice age, both physically, socially, and culturally while living in a barbarous state of filth, savagery, decadence and disease in Europe. Suddenly, you discover that the rest of the world has gone on to form highly advanced civilizations. Build monuments that are the greatest testimony to mans achievement, even today. You discover that the people who accomplished this are black skinned and look nothing like you. Even the lands themselves outside of Europe are warm and rich with an abundance of natural wealth. In essence you have discovered that the rest of the world has completely overshadowed all that you believe yourself to be. You realize that if someone were to compare your development to that of the rest of the world, they would obviously judge you to be a barbarian. What would you then do? You would realize that the evolutionary time clock, for whatever reason, had stopped turning for you long ago. You would realize that at this late stage of the game it is too difficult to make up lost time by honest hard work. Therefore you would simply resort to your naturally barbarous nature to conquer, rape, steal, enslave, and attempt to rewrite history. All in the desperate effort to cover up your lack of evolution, and create a niche in a world that passed you by long ago.

Whites' inferiority complex and natural desire to survive compels them to perpetrate absurd actions that indicate their desperation and frantic struggle for existence. From the beginning of their quest to jockey for position in the world arena, they have always resorted to desperate unorthodox measures to achieve their goals. They have given justification for nothing that they have done other than having a blank check to do what they wish since there is no one to oppose or challenge them. The worst crimes by whites have naturally been against blacks, since we are the group positioned directly opposite them in appearance and nature. Whites commit their crimes against blacks out of fear, envy, frustration and ignorance. Whites realize again that blacks are the one people on the planet who can wipe out any trace of white existence without committing physical murder. Whites have envied the soul, spirituality, and oneness that blacks have with the environment since the days that the Greeks envied and stole the teachings and philosophies of the Egyptians. The natural inability of whites to truly master these disciplines or even compete and participate in popular culture with blacks, causes their frustration and they lash out in envy. Whites work themselves into a mystified stupor when they realize that 40% of black males are involved in the criminal justice system, yet and still we dominate popular culture and sports.

The white race most certainly has its share of problems. As stated, the psyche of the white man is not in the most stable of conditions. This is evident from his use of illusion and other tactics to cover up his inadequacies. The white race is, in actuality, not a unified race. They have a unified consciousness and character, however, their "look out for number one" nature will not allow them to be completely cohesive. Whites are so aggressive in their avarice for resources that they often will step over one another in order to seek advantage. The parasitic nature of whites is clearly evident when it comes to high-level control issues that almost always seem to be related to money and turf. Whites are well aware of their own capabilities and their advantage seeking nature.

The purely schizophrenic behavior of whites is evidence enough to indicate their sick state of being. How could any people go to the beach with the sole intent of darkening their skin, and then scorn another people who are blessed naturally with the condition that they wish to emulate?! Their frustration intensifies when nature denies them what they seek, and inflicts them with skin cancer instead. How could any people call themselves creatures of God, and commit the crimes that they have, in direct conflict with what is taught in their religious doctrines? Why is it that whites acknowledge blacks that they work with on a regular basis in the work environment, yet won't recognize those same individuals on the street? Their behavior is different when in public because publicly all blacks are grouped, labeled, and treated the same. This sad behavior can take on a deadly meaning since quite a few black plain clothed police officers have been shot by their white coworkers outside the office.

The posture that whites have adopted is a function of their innate survival instinct. For example, white supremacy is not a well-defined rigid plan to denigrate other people just for the sake of being cruel. It is a tactic of survival. They proclaim their superiority and hope to persuade the weak minded of the validity of this proclamation, or bully people into conceding that whites are indeed superior. Why is it that white evil still exists and will never die unless put to sleep? Realize that the classic form of slavery ended just a minute ago and has been replaced with its economic brother. During slavery, over 130 million lives were estimated lost in transit to this country. This does not include the millions that died upon arrival. To this day we still have hate groups, discrimination, and a constant desire by law makers to turn back the hands of time. These are the indicators of this groups desperate efforts to survive and the frustration they feel as their attempts fail. Whites have paid a price for their desire to survive, dominate and control. The price is their souls. Whites have subdued their souls to the extent that they cannot feel them nor utilize them to act like creatures of conscience. To give off an air of control and authority whites have socialized themselves into believing that emotion and feelings are signs of weakness and a lack of control. As a result, they have subdued that which makes all of us human. .

Identity Crisis

These people are pitted against the world regarding the definition of their identity. They look in the mirror to this day, and are unsure of what it is exactly that they see. They cannot comprehend why it is that their physical appearance is so drastically different from the majority population of the earth. They are confused as to what their true origin, history, and culture are. The reason that whites gravitate to other cultures and adopt so many of their practices is because they have no cultural basis of their own to reference. This has made them the great emulators and imitators of our time. Most cultures on this earth have rich histories of accomplishment socially, as well as in the sciences and arts. Each culture has made a unique contribution to the continuum of humanity. Whites have merely taken from that continuum, and used its resources to build a history of false accomplishment.

Whites have looked out at the world and its many diverse cultures whose accomplishments make whites look pale in comparison. Sorry. For what ever reason, the world kept spinning while whites were dwelling in caves during their ice age hibernation. Civilizations and rich cultures formed outside of Europe. Monuments that are a testament to mans' ability were erected. Whites eventually woke up, in all their savage splendor. They proceeded on a quest to claim all that they had no part in building. They were also searching for some distant sign of themselves. Some presence that was recognizable outside of Europe. They found nothing. This lead to the early development of an inferiority complex and they proceeded to define themselves at the expense of other civilizations. When something was found that was attractive, they stole it and renamed it. If they found something that they had no ability to understand they destroyed it. When the story was told of how they laid claim to land outside of Europe, they lied for God and Queen.

They continue to search the heavens and earth in order to lay claim to the environment. They build for the future by leaving something behind that they can later recognize. It's like carving your initials into a tree or leaving defecate behind to mark your territory. Whites have left junk on the moon, in space, and under the ocean. They figure that history will not pass them by again if they can leave behind as many footprints as possible in as many places as possible. They have no concern for what gets trampled in the process. Their method of discovery is by dissection and destruction. Whatever it is that they discover they attempt to take it apart in order to comprehend its existence and use its components. This method of discovery usually results in the destruction of the subject that is being "discovered." Millions of people in Africa, the Americas, and around the world owe their near extinction to the privilege of being discovered by the Europeans.

Burden of Legitimization

After having ripped up the world for greed and profit, murdering and enslaving millions, how do you explain yourself? Better yet, how do you sleep with yourself at night? Many whites today say that "I didn't own slaves," and "I'm not responsible for what went on in the past." Yet and still they have benefited from the legacy of slavery. You will not see them turning in their comfortable life styles or dispensing with their general plantation mentality. Whites today want to forget the past and move on because they find themselves having to answer for a great deal. Whites have to bare a burden of legitimization to account for their current status. Declaring yourself superior brings with it an inherent burden. You must maintain your illusion of superiority and convince others that they are inferior.

In order to perpetuate a lie of superiority, whites must convince themselves of their natural superiority and convince nonwhites of their natural inferiority. This is attempted by degrading and dehumanizing nonwhites. If a nonwhite can be portrayed as an animal, it is plausible that they receive treatment deserving of an animal. This is the intention behind those racist jokes that whites love to engage in. Through the usage of such jokes they legitimize their racist treatment of others while reinforcing their false self concept. Whites also like to humiliate nonwhite cultures by using them to suit their own warped purposes. There are quite a few sports teams with Native American names as well as teams with names such as bulldogs, wild cats, and buffaloes. However, they are all considered animals. Whites have classified nonwhite parts of the world as non-industrialized or third world. Often when they show these parts of the world they show the most impoverished scenes that they can find. They depict these regions as backward and lacking of the intelligence to improve their condition. What they fail to state is that many areas of the world are third world because they have been raped of their resources by the West.

Not only can whites make others feel inferior by blatantly denigrating them, but they can accomplish the same goal by ignoring them all together. Whites will often ignore the accomplishments of nonwhites as an attempt to devalue these accomplishments. The history of blacks in particular has been ignored, and as a result we have lost our ties to the past. Many of us have no self esteem because we assume that we have no history of accomplishment. In school we were filled with western civilization as though it is the only history worthy of discussion. A former secretary of education said that "since we are living in western society, that is the history that should be taught in the schools." Those that share this ignorant point of view would love to erase black history if given the opportunity. If an event in black history was monumental enough that it could not be ignored, it was distorted and credited to whites.

Whites validate themselves and their actions by making their images common place and easily accessible as a frame of reference. Whites have perpetuated and inundated us with their images through their use of the media. Many of us have forgotten what we look like until we look in the mirror. White images are everywhere. We see them in the movies, television, magazines and billboards. They project themselves in this manner until they are ingrained in our psyches. This psychological warfare has detrimental effects on all who are forced to endure its attack. Many of us have grown uncomfortable with our appearance and as a result have nurtured the seeds of self hate.

Whites can give validity to anything that they choose through deceptive PR and propaganda. The open celebration of white criminals is so evident, that it is as though whites are flaunting their status by perpetrating outrageous actions without the threat of repercussions. The barbarous legacy and nature of whites are celebrated with total disregard for lawfulness or humanity. The vehicle that allows this is the ignorance of the masses and their lack of power to effect change. The largest monument erected to a white criminal is the Washington monument. An African monument erected to a white man who owned slaves. Go figure. We also have other criminals that adorn our money like Jefferson and Jackson. We have barbarous Columbus who murdered millions, and this man has his own holiday. Whereas someone such as Martin Luther King who tried to show whites how to be civilized, and was murdered for it, required a fight to obtain a holiday to honor him. Then we have the glorification of white barbarism in the movies. We have Rambo, 007, John Wayne, The Godfather, Dirty Harry, Robin Hood, etc.. It is all made OK by conditioning peoples minds to accept the evil nature of whites as standard behavior.

Whites have made it a point to measure everyone against the standards that they have instituted. It gives them the home field advantage and makes everyone else question their natural abilities.

We have books today that dictate our value, intelligence, and future potential based on IQ examinations. They show that we lag behind other racial groups, whites in particular, in IQ scores. What they don't say is that the test is bias and whites have historically retarded our educational development, from forbidding us to read to Brown vs. the Topeka board of education. Once again they attempt to poke our eyes out and later condemn us for being blind. If whites can statistically show that we are inferior, they will justify their malicious treatment of us and convince others that we are unworthy of being treated as humans.

Whites have always instituted a standard to force others to live by. The most obvious standard is their monetary standard that has enslaved and disenfranchised millions to this day. Their standards of beauty continue to confuse those of us who are not self-aware. By our unquestioned acceptance of white standards, we participate in legitimizing their authority over us. We also participate in our own mental captivity. If we continue to live by and perpetuate white standards, we cannot hope for any improvement in our condition, nor that of the world we live in. We are easily asked to forget the past, but we must remember that there is no statute of limitations on murder in any court in the land.

The burden of legitimization is a self-imposed burden that whites are forced to carry. Every day is a balancing act for whites to maintain their self-proclaimed status while convincing nonwhites to accept white standards. This burden forces whites to define their identity by any means at their disposal. In its most extreme case it has resulted in war. Not long ago a small German nation led by a mad man came one breath away from ruling the world and wiping out its nonwhite inhabitants. This same desire for legitimization and identity currently lives in that nation once again and in many other white countries around the world. This burden forces whites to lie to themselves and causes other internal conflicts. When they themselves do not live up to their standards or are found in a subservient position to a nonwhite, they experience an inner struggle. When they highlight blond hair and blue eyes as the standard of beauty, yet still covet the features of black women, it causes internal turmoil. These people realize that the self-imposed burden of living a lie brings with it a high price. It can be summed up by saying that the slave could always manage a little song, while master came down with ulcers worrying about maintaining authority, control, oppressing and making a profit.

Denial

As a result of their burden, and the desire to continue their oppression, whites manifest the psychological condition of denial. This condition sustains their justification of selfish action. In order to treat a sickness, one must first admit that one is sick. Whites have experienced no such revelation and continue to ignore the signs of their illness. Whites do not consider themselves a factor when trying to determine the problems of society. It is a given that societal problems cannot be the fault of whites since their inflated self image tells them that they can do no wrong. When analyzing society for problems, looking in the mirror is not a consideration for whites. It must be someone else. Affirmative action, amendments to the constitution, equal housing, fair employment practices and all the mechanisms that attempt to establish some equitable balance in our society, are in actuality attempts to cure the white sickness of racism. Yet this white disease is never mentioned along with its symptoms and effects. The problem is painted out to be something that is shared by society or a particular community, when in actuality the problem belongs to whites exclusively.

Whites have the ability to look only at problems as they arise. The most visible symptom of a problem draws their attention. They do this because they realize that the root cause of many of today's societal ills can be attributed to whites and their actions. Therefore whites feel the need to shift blame to the individuals who usually happen to be the victims. Using the drug trade as an example, recall when president Bush appeared on television for a press conference holding a bag of crack cocaine. He stated that it had just been seized outside the White House from a drug dealer. The President then continued to talk about crime and drugs in the streets running rampant. He did this because it was the most accessible topic and obvious problem. Naturally he would never talk about the high-level whites who import, transport, and distribute drugs to our community. This is because firstly they are white, and secondly, they have a great deal of money, and as a result command political clout. Whites even have the nerve to place different laws on the books for their drugs of choice. The white drug of choice, cocaine, usually carries a lighter sentence than the inner city drug, crack, which is derivative of cocaine.

Whites also make issue of the hot topic of welfare. Whites will focus on tax dollars that subsidize the lives of blacks because they don't care for blacks anyway. It doesn't matter that there are more poor whites than blacks. Blacks are the most visibly poor people due to their race and over exposure in the media. The media portrays us as the poster children of poor America. They paint a picture of us breeding in the ghettos like so many rats. Instead of focusing on larger issues where whites are to blame for misleading the country, such as fiscal responsibility, the S&L crisis, the ridiculous defense budget, the CIA acting as a separate government, etc. Whites want to focus on people that are barely surviving as the cause of Americas problems. Why? Because it takes the light off of the true white perpetrators of the crimes of greatest magnitude. If it weren't true, it would be one hilarious joke. Whites, in their blind quest for the source of today's problems, have even suggested funding for research to study the relationship between ethnic background and violence. They would love to discover that blacks are naturally prone toward violence. Can you imagine white people telling us that *WE* are prone toward violence? One does not put a people in bondage, steal their land, and rape their women simply with harsh language.

The inherent state of denial that white people experience is truly fascinating. These people can place another people in bondage, quote scripture, and name their slave ships The Jesus all in the same breath. Their most violent hate groups can burn crosses in the yard of any hard working citizen. Whites can arm a foreign country, plunge it into civil war, pull out, let its people starve, and then come back to play hero, only to pull out again and let the people starve some more. There are no arms or drug manufacturers in the inner city, yet and still whites believe that the problems are located there.

The cowardice of denial is also fascinating. They still hide behind sheets. They hide behind offices, behind language, in suburban homes, in their church, and behind their ignorance. They hide from interaction that may lead them to discover that they are dealing with other humans. It is difficult to perpetrate a crime against someone that you've come to know. They must maintain a distance so that human emotions do not impede their selfish actions.

The reason that they run from black history is because it is to humiliating for them to face and it would humanize black people. If our true story was ever told, it would be an indefensible indictment against whites. Even to this day when they hear of their past crimes, they are embarrassed and want to hide in humiliation. They grow tired of hearing how evil they are and want to silence those who speak the truth. The monumental scale of their crime seems too fantastic to be believable and they dismiss it with an uncomfortable laugh. They also tell themselves that they owe us nothing today. The vehemence of their denial is all the more indication of their guilt.

When progress is made toward gaining true human rights, it amazes me how whites like to take pride in saying that things are getting so much better. Again, some whites of conscience do take part in progress, however the vast majority are the self-absorbed idiots who must be shown how doggish and devilish they are. It becomes necessary to go to court and prove their evil by means of the laws they themselves have established. Whites hate it when you can throw something back in their faces that they had originally written to afford themselves advantage. We are left with the burden of having to punch holes in their ignorance.

26

Insecurity and Fear

There can be no other explanation for some of the stupid and childish actions perpetrated by white people. Many of their deeds seem like those of an 8th grade bully. Bullies usually turn out to be insecure individuals hiding their short comings under a mask of toughness and authority through intimidation. They need constant reassurance of their status as the biggest kids on the block. They expel a great deal of effort to keep others down to protect their false sense of security and control. Even the most liberal white is comfortable with blacks advancing but so far. Whites fight a battle against reality and time; both will eventually betray them.

There is an unnerving similarity in the manner that people of color are treated by whites in all parts of the world and in every major city in America. Whites usually make it a point to keep blacks in a controllable position. From South Africa to Southern France to Southern Chicago, blacks are systematically placed in environments where their actions are observable, controllable and isolated. Blacks, as well as the world in which we exist is held hostage and kept in a state of imbalance. These artificial conditions are imposed to afford advantage to those seemingly in control. Imbalance and displacement are whole scale industries. The drug trade, arms manufacturing, war, are all trillion dollar businesses based on taking advantage of those that do not have the wherewithal to withstand the imposition. Those engaged in projecting their wills to impact the environment do so out of a desire for control and a false feeling of authority. Whites feel that if they do not subject the environment to their wishes, it could mean that their handle on the world may escape them. This would result in their destruction or assimilation and the end to western civilization. These dreaded fears are the reason that the white man clutches to his weapons of destruction so tightly and has forced himself to forever sleep with one eye open.

The effort expended to maintain a choke hold on the world and people of color is not only neurotic, but it is a waste of resources.

EON

The white male's self-imposed burden of structuring civilization to provide himself with unfair and undeserved advantage is totally unnecessary. The fact that whites would rather spend three times as much money to jail an individual than to educate or rehabilitate one, is a symptom of their sickness. They would rather spend money to sweep you out of sight and into a controlled environment, than deal with you as a human being. When you believe that you have forced them to respect you because of your qualifications and hard work, they will in turn find a way to denigrate you. Perhaps by calling you "affirmative action baby" or other such label. These kinds of comments are meant to kill the spirit and bring about feelings of futility in attempting any sort of achievement. It is simply the frustrated name calling of a bully. Whites attempts to sabotage the achievements of others and ignore the achievement of others is not only wasted effort, it serves to hold back the whole of humanity. Their selfish actions do all of us, including themselves, a disservice. Their preoccupation with structure, authority, and control is a burden that will eventually consume them.

Arrogance of Ignorance

I usually have the ability to not let the inherent insensitivity and seemingly intentional evil of some white people get to me. However, the one aspect of whites that tightens my jaws is their incredible arrogance derived from their perpetual and self-imposed state of ignorance. It is so ingrained in them that they are superior by divine nature, that these people exhibit a God complex. Whites ride the deceptive PR and propaganda campaign of life in an effort designed to validate all that they believe themselves to be, and all that they want others to believe them to be. They have rewritten the past as well as distorted the present. Whites will create a perception of nonwhites as being inferior because it gives whites something to look down on while elevating their own status. It is a matter of perspective. In order to know that one is moving forward, one must look at someone that is either standing still or moving backward. As an example, let's look at the way in which whites have attempted to portray the colonists that "discovered" this country. I was taught, in my white public school system, that these people were honorable Europeans seeking freedom from persecution. Although they were seeking freedom, in actuality these people were the vilest scum that Europe had to offer. They brought with them diseases and animals that killed millions in the Americas and it is my understanding that many relationships were consummated between *ALL* the passengers during these long, lonely voyages. Once in America these people enslaved others to do their work to alleviate them of their own retched status.

An attitude of superiority has been ingrained in whites over a long period of time. The attitude of whites reminds me of a high school football cheer I once heard where the winning team taunted their opponents by yelling "Look at the score board, Look at the score board...." Whites have smugly been saying "look at the score board" for quite some time even though they have scored no legitimate points of which to boast. They have always been the standard setters and law givers based on the fact that, at this juncture, they are winning the game in some respects. Their self-proclaimed status is further elevated by those surrounded by the white world who are forced to concede to its standards due to lack of power. We are forced to wear European clothes, speak English, see our culture corrupted and trashed for monetary profit, and call ourselves by foreign names, all in an effort to assimilate and survive. Yet we will never be seen as equal because whites must step on other cultures in order to elevate themselves since their culture cannot stand on its own merit due to its nonexistence.

These people believe that they are in a position to critique the whole of society. Something has been instilled in them that leads them to believe that they are ordained to establish the standards by which we are all to live by and to aspire. They feel as though they are in a position to establish a schedule and timetable for my and your advancement; that they can state what is intended "for us" and what is not. Whites have always placed themselves in a position to validate or invalidate nonwhite cultures. The world and its many already existing civilizations were not discovered until the Europeans came out of their ice age exile to discover them. It's as though we are pledging their fraternal organization and we must continually seek their guidance and approval if we are to be considered for admittance. They love to speak of the first black to do "so and so" as if we have finally proven ourselves worthy of their company. In actuality due to their ignorance, elitism, and assumptions made about other peoples' character and abilities, there are quite a few firsts that should have happened long ago. It is infuriating when they remove their policies of exclusion, and turn around to say that "times are getting better" and "blacks are making progress." This implies that we are making progress toward attaining the high, lofty standards that whites have set for us, and they have finally decided to allow us to merge into the privileged mainstream. They will also play themselves on the other side of the equation and act as though they are actively taking part in the solutions of our problems. Granted, some whites of good nature are actually of assistance. However, other less sincere whites simply want to keep and eye on us and remove the satisfaction we gain from solving our own problems.

Due to the severity of their ignorance, their education is a current topic of hot discussion. They need sensitivity training, diversity training, and tolerance training. This is actually anti-white male ignorance training. They cleverly attempt to educate the rest of us along with them, so as to take light off of the extent of their ignorance. We all have to take diversity training that is simply Respect 101 or the old values of our black culture. They speak of racial tolerance as though we are so different and substandard that they need be tolerant of us and put up with our presence. They also have sensitivity training. I don't need this and neither do they. I don't want their damn sensitivity as though I'm some child who needs to be catered to and pampered. All I desire is their respect, and I'm prepared to take that if they don't give it willingly. All these efforts are, in actuality, politically based. Companies and organizations institute these training programs so that when these employment lawsuits come up, their organizations, as a whole, are not held responsible. They can say, "I don't understand so and so's actions. We have had sensitivity training and done all that we can on the part of the organization." Whites, as a whole, really have no desire to become more educated or familiar with nonwhites. Whites desire to remain largely ignorant and insensitive. It gives them license to perpetrate their actions and maintain their distance from nonwhites. It's simpler to discriminate against someone with whom you are unfamiliar. It's also hard to perpetrate a crime against another perceived human of equal value. Even in the indirect sense, whites do not want to discover that the rest of us are, in actuality, human beings. This is the reason that blacks cannot land many dramatic roles in the movies and television. We are portrayed as thugs, drug addicts, whores, and comedic buffoons. This makes whites comfortable. They can justify their racist actions toward us as a function of the images with which they have programmed themselves.

Another issue of late that white males are promoting with vigor is that of family values. The conservative political right has really latched on to this topic. For some inexplicable reason, I find their crusade on this issue particularly insulting, since a white male talking about family values is like a counterfeiter talking about the value of the dollar. After all, it was a white male son-of-a-bitch who broke my black family up in the first place in order to make a buck. I guess disenfranchised families are not as profitable as they once were.

The obvious arrogance of whites is most clearly visible in their actions. One has to laugh out of frustrated anger at these people who believe they can continue to operate with impunity yet impose their double standards on others. The one aspect of white arrogance that is most annoying is the process of raping other cultures to serve white purposes. This action by whites demonstrates their complete insensitivity and disregard for those who are different from themselves, as well as their ignorance concerning the nature of what they target for exploitation. Since whites have demonstrated little culture and creativity of their own, they must adopt and dilute other cultures to suit their needs. Whites have been stealing the accomplishments of other peoples for so long that whites can literally steal a concept, perhaps add a minor twist, and sincerely believe that they are the originators of that concept. Whites still utilize all the tools at their disposal to lay claim to that which could never be theirs. Whites believe that statues such as the Washington monument are symbols of white culture and accomplishment. These ignorant people add insult to the meaning of this strictly African creation by utilizing it as the male phallic symbol to white power. Whites also utilize the movie industry to lay claim to that which does not belong to them. When the movie "10" opened with actress Bo Derrick, white women thought that they had invented a new original hair style in the form of braids. This regardless of the fact that African women originated this hair style and have been wearing them for thousands of years. A more contemporary example of white culture rape is evident in the music industry. Whites continue to fabricate their own music icons in an effort to carve out their niche by any means other than hard work and true talent. Michael Bolton, who has zero talent, was recently in court for his theft of black music. It should be no surprise that he lost the case. Probably the greatest fabricated white music legend is that of Elvis as the king of Rock and Roll. Whites generally feel admiration for other cultures. Especially black culture. However, how can you tell a people that they are great and maintain your control over them? As a result whites create people such as Elvis to legitimize white infatuation with other cultures and make themselves more comfortable with that which is not naturally theirs. They also avoid having their little white girls swoon over black entertainers such as Nat King Cole, who incidentally was run out of town by white men when this happened. In the case of Elvis, the true architects of Rock and Roll (Little Richard, Chuck Berry, Fats Domino and many others) had their work stolen, corrupted, made a little tighter, a little whiter, and put out as a product for white consumers. Whites could not possibly have their daughters idolizing black male rock stars. I also find it amazing that whites have tried to convince the general populous, with much success, that Rock is a form of white music. They can only do this since they have Elvis to downplay the black founding fathers of this musical art form. All this in spite of the fact that Jimmy Hendrix was the greatest Rock and Role performer of all time.

In the recent past, we had a brief surge of white rappers. I don't know where they all went, but I suppose their lack of talent eventually caught up with them. I love this subject. It displays white rape, arrogance, envy, and schizophrenia. They even attempted to create another white music icon, Vanilla Ice; his name alone makes issue of his whiteness and implied superiority. It is an example of what I will call the modern day *Tarzan Syndrome* and the definition of what can be considered "white chic." The Tarzan Syndrome has the symptoms of a white man in a jungle like atmosphere temporally adopting the ways of the animals to display his skills as far as survival and flexibility. As a result whites prove their superiority by adapting to that which is considered foreign, yet maintain their whiteness first and foremost. The white definition of chic is derived from their eclectic nature. They figure that if one can take a piece of another culture and claim to understand that culture, one is seen as hip and versatile amongst ones' peers. You prove your superiority by being able to transform out of your white face and perform with those who consider their abilities uniquely special. Vanilla Ice is an example of the stagnant condition of whites and exemplifies an aspect of their character that will not change. He was successful because whites will always embrace their great white hopes. However, with blacks he was seen for what he was, a floundering white boy with no rhyme scheme, rhythm or soul. The true schizophrenia of white rappers was evidenced by some of them arguing amongst one another about black cultural authenticity. They were upset with people like Vanilla because he was too commercial and diverged from the roots of true rap. It is amazing. These people are not only arrogant, they are downright stupid.

Whites don't have the ability to relate well with that which is nonwhite in nature. They find the need to rename things to make themselves feel comfortable. Whites will usually mispronounce ethnic names with a "proper" English version. You will find people with extremely ethnic names being called Bob, John, or Jack, and willingly submitting to this mistreatment all with the hope of being accepted. As far as names are concerned, white arrogance is at its peak when naming its sports teams after Native Americans. Whites will actually try to rationalize that these names are "honoring our native Americans," as one white team owner put it. When in actuality it is just another form of white rape. The rape of the Native American name began all the way back with stupid ass Columbus. He named the inhabitants of this land Indians because the dumb bastard actually thought that he landed in India, his intended destination. At any rate, since Native Americans do not command the economic, political, and social clout to gain the respect of whites, they are culturally raped. As a result, we have the sports teams such as the Atlanta Braves, the Cleveland Indians, the Florida Seminols and worst of all, the Washington Redskins blatantly named after a peoples skin color. Whites could not hope to have a culture as rich as the Native American, therefore they rape and paint an inferiority picture of the these great people to demonstrate their false cultural dominance. They hope that the true bravery and honor of Native Americans will not be discovered as whites continue to carve out their illegitimate niche at the expense of other peoples. Pontiac is not a damn car, it's a Native American chief. Even the white monster Hitler felt the need to steal his so called swastika from the Native American.

If one were to ask whites who built this country, they would naturally reply with perceived honesty, the white founding fathers: Washington, Jefferson, etc. This, with total disregard that this country was built on the backs of millions of slaves many of which were murdered in the middle passage to this great land. Just think,

400 years of free labor. Yet whites overlook this to highlight their contribution that is indeed negligible unless one considers the work of murdering and enslaving millions hard work. Whites will again say, "I'm not responsible for what was done in the past." If a white person lives off of an actual fortune or the environment that was created by a legacy such as slavery, they also have blood on their hands. Some whites would like to be cleared of their past transgressions, but if that meant giving up advantage and privilege in today's world, they will simply remain bloody. They want to enjoy the fruit even though they were not the ones to shake the tree. They are the ultimate example of hypocrisy and arrogance who will shroud themselves in the flag or the bible to cloak their true nature and hide their ignorance.

When the Illusion Fails...

Whites must stick to what they believe regardless of what reality dictates since truth has historically proven to be the enemy of the white man. Whites are faced with their inadequacies on a daily basis from their pale physical appearance to their inability to compete in popular culture and sports. If whites were indeed superior they would show no fear of competition from others. An example of welcoming competition would be as follows: a group of black males are on a basketball court engaged in a game when some white boys approach and ask if they can play the winners. The brothers would naturally accept the challenge and no doubt try to put some money on the game, knowing that, "Ain't no white boys gonna take a group of brothers on the blacktop." Blacks recognize their dominance and superior skills in basketball and welcome open competition based on self-confidence and pure competitive spirit. On the slanted white basketball court, the converse is not true. Whites are continually shown that they are not superior when they swing the doors of opportunity open. When they decide to be adventurous and open these doors, they are confronted face to face with their own inadequacies. They realize immediately that anytime whites do not control the factors surrounding a particular event such as the rules and venue, they are at a natural disadvantage.

In order to protect the few venues that deal to some degree with physicality, whites attempt to dissuade blacks from participation so as to avoid another basketball-like situation. Whites have such an intense fear of being excluded from popular sports that they will voluntarily leave or simply rear their youngsters to participate in other activities such as golf, swimming, and hockey that are not YET popular with blacks. They would rather leave a sport than be humiliated by fair and open competition, the mark of the ultimate coward. Whites will stoop to the desperate measure of creating ridged test environments where blacks are intended to fail in order to validate white superiority and discourage the desire of blacks to participate. Such was the case of the Tuskeegee Airmen where whites set out to prove that black people didn't have the ability to fly airplanes. Naturally these courageous black men made asses out of the conductors of this experiment by flying over 1500 escort missions in W.W.II, without losing a single plane. Such courage was also shown by the Buffalo Soldiers, Fighting 54, and 761st Tank Battalion. Whites understand what happens when blacks are allowed to openly participate. The white contribution is significantly decreased along with the myth of white superiority.

The white man continues to be confronted with his own ever more obvious inadequacies and complexes. The white man will always feel dogged by the sexuality of the black male and the indisputable genetic dominance of the black male. The white mans reaction in an effort to confront this inferiority complex accounts for his disdain and loathing of the black male. In body building, a sport that is based on pure physical development, whites have to contend with Lee Haney as the greatest body builder of all time overshadowing the Terminator, Arnold Schwarzenegger. Whites in boxing are a non-issue. If you will observe you will see that white men, confronted by their physical inadequacy, enjoy activities that remove a great deal of the physicality. They enjoy sports that utilize tools that don't require a great deal of strength such as skiing, golf, tennis, polo, and shooting guns. They also like sports where they can encase themselves in some type of physical exoskeleton to extend the limits of their physical being such as auto racing and flying jet planes. These activities also intended to highlight "superior" skill and intelligence.

Whites must deal with other physical insecurities regarding the changing standards of beauty. No one wants pale skin, and as a result people who suffer from that condition seek to tan. If one takes a look at the glamour and fashion magazines, one will observe white schizophrenia and self hate at its most obvious. This is evidenced by white women who have surgically altered lips thicker than those of black women. The general standards of beauty are turning to people who have pigment, full lips, tight high butts, and accentuated cheek bones. Whites are not satisfied with their physical condition as it compares to other supposed disadvantaged groups. They will go to extreme measures to artificially mimic the characteristics of those whom they consider inferior.

Whites also see the walls closing in on other frontiers. We have many, young, black entertainers rising to superstar status, many of them black males. Even in the back yard of the white man, corporate America, we have minorities and women playing ever increasing roles. It is just a matter of time before the ole boy network and its glass protective ceiling are destroyed. On top of all this, the white man is confronted by the Asians who continue to capture markets. The Japanese rightly called American products inferior, and said that white CEO's earn too much money and take too much vacation. In a situation such as this where the white male is again faced with the truth, he will actually have the gaul to cry foul and arrogantly ask for concessions. This was done with Japan during trade negotiations.

White institutions by nature are transient and fluctuating. They are weak because they lack substance. At the core of their being are their financial institutions. These institutions are characterized by a fragile yet volatile unpredictability. When a white person loses their money, they have lost their soul. They are ostracized by those whom they would call friend and who share the same values. Many commit suicide. Others eventually self-destruct. They believe that they are given purpose by hoarding the earth's resources. When these resources are removed, so is the purpose of the white man.

Whites have looked back at the accomplishments of the ancient world and couldn't find their place. This is similar to their confusion today. The position and posture of white people are based on a lie. They have no pyramids. They have no cultural contributions to the modern world that were not stolen. Even their much revered Greeks were little more than savage barbarians whose philosophers were persecuted by their own people. Yet today they are depicted as the precursors to modern culture. These thieves and murderers were all that the modern white man had to reach out to legitimize his presence today, and even this is a lie. European countries, such as England, today paint themselves out to be the pinnacle of civility by their subjects calling themselves lord, queen and nobleman. They are no more than the murderous, empire building, enslaving, rapists that they have always been. The Egyptians ruled the world for thousands of years because they were the people kissed by the sun and worked as no other people have since. The rule of whites has been but a blink of an eye in comparison, and already we can see their illegitimacy to the throne that they lay claim to in today's society. It is but a matter of time. Their rule cannot last because it is based on a lie, and all lies are exposed and destroyed, just as all great empires both good and bad have fallen.

Tactics: Poke my eyes out and condemn me for being blind

The tactics of oppression used by whites against nonwhites, blacks in particular, are difficult to detect due to their subtle yet bold nature. It is almost inconceivable to try and understand how any people could coordinate efforts that are designed to hold a people back, maintain control over them, and keep them at a desired distance. One must become sensitized to the actions and strategy of whites in order to recognize their aims, fend against their efforts, and truly be in control of one's destiny. Whites have realized that overt racist policy is met with to much galvanized resistance. More clandestine subtle techniques can lull people into a false sense of security where the original aims of the strategy can be more quietly achieved. It is essential for whites to achieve their aims of racism without making to many waves and turning popular sentiment against them in this politically correct age. Those loose white cannons who make waves will be sacrificed or thrown to the lions in order to take attention away from the collective body and the desired goal.

The vehicle that allows whites to achieve their goals in a kinder, gentler manner is their communication. The greatest attribute whites have is their communication amongst one another, and their ability to confuse nonwhites as to what they are actually doing and saying. White communication is so highly developed that they simply have to gesture to one another or allude to one another to convey a meaning. There is never a need to speak directly in plain words whereby one might implicate oneself or others who are aligned with the same cause.

In the not so recent past, whites would use overt brutality and cruelty to show blacks that they were expendable. White slave owners would simply cut the baby from the pregnant slave, or cut the male genitals off in front of the other slaves to demonstrate that their lives had little value. Today, whites use tactics of oppression that allow blacks to draw their own conclusions as to our, allegedly worthless nature and seemingly hopeless condition. These tactics are important to understand and are located in the Appendix in greater detail.

Environment

Creation and manipulation of the environment. The desire of the white male is to control, dominate, and assert himself over the environment. He does this in a manner that displaces others and carves a comfortable niche for himself. The white male desires an environment where he can naturally be seen as master. For this to occur, there must be a self-praising public relations program firmly in place. Physicality cannot be an issue since it's obvious that the white male is not physically superior or otherwise for that matter. The white male must carefully choreograph the supporting characters in his drama since he must always see himself as playing the lead role.

Whites have been at odds with the environment since their emergence from the Ice Age into already existent civilization. They consider the environment an adversary; something to be conquered and exploited for personal gain. The Europeans introduced plant and animal life in places outside of Europe that to this day have thrown entire ecosystems out of balance. Whites adversarial relationship with the environment has lead to the earth's numerous environmental problems as well as the disenfranchisement of many of its people. The cultures of most people of color are based on maintaining a balance and degree of harmony with the environment. Many worshipped the earth's elements; the wind, soil, water, and sun. European culture is based on no such balance. Europeans fought for their survival against the harsh environment of ice age Europe. They were constantly forced by environmental conditions to seek shelter in caves, plant crops on time, and harvest on time in order to survive. As Europeans came into power, they developed the agenda and means by which to dissect the environment for personal advantage. They have created industries to remove the earth's resources, and have forced many of us to become dependent on employment that does the environment grave damage. They have created markets for commodities that continue to rob the earth of its gifts. They have created monetary standards based on precious materials that have forced all of us to take part in the mutual dissection and destruction of the earth. The white male has left garbage in each corner of the environment that he has violated. From the moon, to garbage floating in space, to the pollution of our air, water, and land. The white male has used science to dissect the most fundamental of the earth's components to enslave all of us in a nuclear web of destruction. White males hold, literally, the fate of the Earth and all its people within reach of a button. It's far too scary a prospect to obsess over. However, regardless of outcome, the earth was here before white males, and it will be here long after they are gone. The rest of us will remain to sweep away their ashes forever more.

White males have strategically put themselves in bastions of control that dictate the tone and operation of society. The erection of their ivory towers is the result of their insecure nature and the desire to insulate themselves from those they affect. They insulate themselves by using the language of politicians, corporate executives, police, and the military. Their communication is not meant to convey a meaning or their true intentions. It is designed to convey an illusion of authority and scholarship that justifies their actions. It is meant to blur, confuse, and soften the messages of oppression.

White males feel the need to statistically manipulate us since it is easier to deal with a number than a human being. We all have our SS number, (whose initials take on a rather dubious meaning). We have demographics and census data that describe the profile of society. White males do all that is in their power to remove humanity from the equation; and in essence emotion. It provides them with a license to orchestrate and perpetuate the conditions they impose.

The burden of the white male is the most arrogant, self-imposed burden ever conceived. They actually feel as though the operation of society from its highest function down to our individual lives is left up to their dictates. They refuse to accept that nonwhites and women are fully capable of governing society and their own lives.

EON

They believe that the white male standard is the standard that all people regardless of background, origin, experience, and belief, are expected to follow. This is precisely the ignorance that is smothering the advantages of having many different points of view. This society is inhibited by white males and their forced expectations of the rest of us. Those of us who are self aware realize that no man has true power over another. We are those who are considered threatening, independent, thinkers by white males. We're Newjacks. However, there exists something odd that white males will not admit to. They find those that cannot resist their actions of capitulation weak, unworthy of respect, and undeserving of free will. On the other hand, those that have the capacity to withstand their arrogant dictates, via the strength of their spirit and assertion of manhood, are respected. Even in death.

White males feel as though they are responsible for the composition and makeup of society. They decide who will be the first black or woman to do whatever. Who will advance in what time frame and how many will advance. They project their ignorance of the rights of individuals as some honorable obstacle that other nonwhite males simply have to overcome by remaining overly patient and subservient. They decide where the interests of white males need be represented and where the numbers of white males need be maintained or increased. They consider themselves the master chefs who use the makeup of the earth to concoct their recipe. They believe that they determine the consistency and ingredients of the cake composed of humanity. They forge the diverse ingredients in the fires of ignorance and hate. They then cover everything with the white icing of oppression to make the product appear appetizing and sweet to the taste.

The atmosphere that the white man creates for blacks and women is designed to serve his purposes by giving positive affirmation to his self-proclaimed greatness and superiority. The environments created for both blacks and women are similar in that each individual must conform to predetermined roles they are forced to play. This is due to a lack of power (political and/or economic), to define roles for themselves. The environment dictated by white men for blacks and women does not take into account intelligence, potential, or character. The environment defined for black men in particular dictates that their value rests purely in physicality, just as it did during slavery. Black men are made to realize that their value lies in physical servitude. We have a disproportionate number of black males being denied opportunity so that they can be funneled into the military. We maintain images of black men pitted against one another in the media and for profit in sports; boxing in particular. The general competitive atmosphere that exists among black males is derived from existence in this environment. The atmosphere that the white male has created for the female bases her value on her femininity and sexuality. The white man has funneled women into prostitution, exotic dancing, beauty pageants, miracle bras, and nude magazines. All by denying opportunity, a woman's place and expectations are very clearly defined. Truly attractive women are given a hard time if they chose to be a professional. They are persecuted and driven into exploitive niches by males. If a woman wants serious consideration for advancement up the corporate ladder, she must adopt a white male demeanor of sorts, along with a short snappy haircut to project that androgynous look. If one is black or a woman, one cannot go for more than a few minutes per day without a white male reminding you that you are black or a woman. White males can go through an entire day without paying notice to their physical condition due to lack of oppression from any other segment of our population. As long as the power to define environments exclusively rests with white males, people who do not enjoy their heinous distinction will be forced to sacrifice their dignity and character. If one does not have sufficient power to control their environment, they can be forced to whore, Uncle Tom, sell drugs, and sit by while their culture is raped. All as a means of survival in a white-male dominated society.

Whites as a whole long for an atmosphere where they can just be white (i.e., insensitive, brutal, vile). Where they can tell dry jokes and use racist references without running the risk of being labeled a racist bad guy or being politically incorrect. They crave places such as those country clubs and red neck bars where they don't have to walk their usual daily tight rope worrying about the risk of offending nonwhites. They also want a place where they can reinforce their view of superiority amongst one another. These safe havens are becoming more and more rare. One safe haven of this nature that is under attack is corporate America. Once thought to be the last bastion of white male power, corporate America is now undergoing a transformation. It is a slow transformation since the dress, demeanor, and rules of order are still dictated by white males. However, uncontested white male operation with overt reckless abandon toward others is no longer tolerated. Interestingly enough, in the corporate atmosphere whites themselves are willing to make sacrifices of character in an effort to be a peer member of this society. They will "suck up" to one another without shame because they realize that they will be accepted as peer members of the collective body with all the rights and privileges thereof. They will be members of the frat. Those who are nonwhite can never be accepted, and waste their time in any attempts to that end. Some white women can enjoy a degree of that acceptance at the cost of extreme sacrifice.

It is my belief that white males will restrict the advancement of nonwhite males simply out of instinct. Their inflated self concept does not allow for others to readily advance past them. They will not encourage your advancement nor applaud your efforts toward advancement unless you are accomplishing a milestone well beneath their current status. White males desire a degree of exclusivity. It's their club that gives them a sense of value and belonging. Whites do not appreciate it when blacks achieve the ability to move into their neighborhood. Their exclusivity has been compromised and they can no longer brag to their friends how elite their neighborhood is. They also enjoy the power associated with determining the extent to which people advance. They enjoy the power that they have over those who are employed by white organizations. They enjoy their ability to evaluate us and determine our value in dollars and cents in salary and raises.

The one aspect of the environment that whites are obsessed with controlling is their proximity to nonwhites. Whites are paranoid about being too close to blacks in particular, although they naturally gravitate toward black influences and culture. This natural fascination and attraction could lead to the unthinkable act of a black marrying into a white family. If whites become physically closer to nonwhites, they would eventually realize that nonwhites are human beings. Proximity is indirectly related to money. The more money one possess, the more options and avenues of advancement one has. The reason money is such an issue with whites is because it provides them with their most effective buffer. Money allows them to move into the exclusive neighborhood, join the exclusive club, church, send their kids to private and ivy league schools, and distance themselves from blacks. Whites are very sensitive to discussion of money since whites define themselves by their money. They guard their financial information with the same zeal that they guard the false purity of their race. They have no desire for blacks to ever attain equity with regard to economic means. This would compromise the exclusivity that they have worked to maintain at the expense of others.

The White Collective vs. The Past

The white male and his verbal denial of the past, yet natural attraction to that which he comes from, is an epic struggle that rips at the white male from two opposing directions. The white male in his heart and soul realizes precisely what his relationship is to black African peoples. He doesn't need the irrefutable evidence that life began in Africa and that which he came from was a black man and woman. Whites know this to be true as they search their hardened hearts. A white males past manifests itself every time that he looks at a black person and takes notice of the drastic differences between themselves. The white male, in order to legitimize his presence and physical appearance, knows that he can never identify with those that he must say are inferior. He must separate himself from his past to the best of his ability by denying the place that Africa holds as the mother of humanity and civilization. The white male could never acknowledge this fact since it would take away from his very being and remove all the advantages that go along with being white and elite. The white male does not want to deal with his true history nor does he desire to learn black history. He fears he would discover that the place of whites in history was stolen through deception and brutality. If it were generally known that white civilization lived in Europe in caves like barbarians, while Africa developed highly modern and structured society, the entire white illusion would crumble and fail. This is why whites utilize selective avoidance and short-term memory regarding all things related to Africa. Maintaining a lie is an incredible burden for the white male and he will often exhibit behavior that indicates the stress of supporting this repression and denial.

It is simple to observe whites openly conceding some of the battles that they wage between their black past and white present. Why is it that white people tan? It is because they realize that having pigment or melanin in the skin is a natural condition that nature forces them to simulate. Only in death do people become pale and lifeless. Color is a natural condition of that which is vibrant and living. We're called 'hue'mans for a reason. Whites resent blacks because blacks don't have to go to these lengths to look natural and human. That's why they can leave the beach after hours of baking and still call you nigga. Whites desire to tan is equivalent to their desire to go back to what they once were. It is like fish attempting to return to their spawning ground. The only problem is that they will never win the fight against up stream waters with skin cancerous undercurrents.

Why is it that white males have such a fascination and longing for black females? They have a desire to return back to the mother they were born of. This desire can be plainly seen as a prominent aspect of history if you would today simply compare the complexions of your five closest black friends. White males most actively pursue their desire to return to mother Africa through their sexual longing for black women. Why is it that whites are so fascinated by black culture and attempt to adopt, emulate, or mutate parts of it? Again, it's their natural longing for the past that is manifesting itself.

History. Enemy of the white man. How does he cope? He copes through short-term memory and a lack of concern for the accumulated waste that is a byproduct of white progress. Whites live for today; they say that this is the society that we live in currently and to hell with the past. Whites don't want to hear anything related to African history nor the white legacy of brutality throughout history. Today is the only day that has meaning. It doesn't matter that slavery is the system that made this country strong, or that this country benefited from a free labor system that placed inhuman demands on its workers. What matters is that we are here today and white people are at the controlling tiers of our society, sitting relatively pretty. Whites today will say, with unbelievable honesty, that they took no part in the past. Their linear interpretation of time is ideal to separate themselves from their past crimes. This is regardless of the fact that the legacy of those crimes has set the stage for their current attitude and actions. Whites are so detached from history that when a barbarism such as slavery is brought up, it seems like a joke or a consideration that should not be addressed in this day and age. Whites feel as though they have done enough for us and are sick and tired of hearing how evil they are and have been in the past. Any mention of programs that are designed to correct the white sickness of their past transgressions is not acceptable today, because yesterday is a non-issue that should be left alone. They don't like affirmative action or welfare because whites are not being afforded advantage; even though the majority of welfare recipients are white. When they see the ghettos of urban America, they feel nothing. No remorse for their part in creating that condition, no sorrow for those that exist in that state, nothing. As long as those issues do not impact white people or their communities on this day, to hell with the past legacy that created these conditions.

The white male today is confronted with having to deal with the byproducts of his "progress." The white male wishes that the black slaves that he used to build this country could have been thrown away like so much utter trash. Essentially they were by being made into economic slaves with no power to improve their condition. However, we are still here and the white collective is confronted with having to find new ways (environments) to sweep us under the rug. The white collective expends much effort to control those that it considers garbage instead of considering the benefits of recycling the most recyclable of all resources, human resources. The white man's ego and superior view of self could mean the economic failure and general deterioration of this country and many others.

Present day whites are still as brutal as their not so distant ancestors. Do we actually believe that these people have evolved so far in such a short period of time as man has been on the earth? Look at the present barbarous conditions in Europe. You have Neo-Nazis that still worship Hitler and deny that the Holocaust ever happened, perhaps the worst case of short- term memory on record. You have ethnic fighting throughout Europe. Even Russia has awakened and is trying to change its slave society because it didn't work. Here in America we practiced legalized apartheid up until about 30 years ago and its legacy lives on. The cold and selfish attitude of the white collective has evolved little since their cave dwelling days. They don't realize that their natural gravitation toward blacks and our culture could transcend their racism and lead the way to the discovering of their souls. Their inflated self concept and ignorance stand in the way.

Socialized Tight Asses

Are these people as rigid, soulless, tight ass, plain, bland and lacking as they appear, or are they playing a well-choreographed role? Have you ever noticed how people in positions of authority cannot appear informal? They must appear to be the staunch general, executive, or football coach on the sidelines showing no emotion, the pinnacle of restraint and superior thinking. They put on their conservative European suits with their ties tied up to their neck tightly in an inhibited, constipated, British manner. This is the role that whites have defined for themselves. As a result, the white male has socialized himself to a point that he cannot readily recognize his soul unless it is down on paper in black and white. I like to call them "the paper people." If something is not documented it has no meaning and whites cannot act accordingly. We have the Constitution, all the other laws on the books, we have legal contracts, one cannot advance in this society without the proper paper credentials (i.e., diploma). We cannot even leave the country without a passport. Their language has no color and is put together in rigid fashion. They express confusion when they cannot understand some type of non-standardized communication. The slang that blacks use has always made them crazy. If the form of communication is not well defined and documented, whites will usually not understand.

Whites can dissect the science of the pyramid and discover that the ratio of its dimensions is equivalent to π, or that the structure itself is aligned to within seconds of true north, but they have not the soul to begin to duplicate such a feet from conception to completion. Whites have always used some baseline or starting point upon which to build their accomplishments. They get gun powder from the Chinese and invent the cannon to conquer. They kidnap slaves that built a great civilization in Africa to build one in America. The Greeks needed to steal the knowledge of the Egyptians in order to take credit for the founding of medicine, science, religion, government, and philosophy. Whites needed blacks to create Rock,

Jazz, R&B, and Rap. Then they created Elvis to lay claim to the music before this accomplishment, like all others preceding it, escaped the participation of whites.

Whites take things in their most literal sense. For whites, if it is written down and documented it must be valid. They will only show signs of change if you show them by means of their own documentation that they are engaged in wrong doing. It is always required that the standards that they have developed be the basis upon which society is judged. They will answer to no higher authority than their own. Therefore they continually attempt to refine their guidelines to afford themselves advantage.

Whites inhibited persona does them a great deal of damage when they are encountered with something that they have not managed to corrupt or control. They do not have an ability to deal with the unorthodox, or that which has not been quantized, quantified, and analyzed. They have a great deal of trouble understanding spirituality and that which goes beyond the physical. Often times their methodology and systems are reasons that they inflict damage on nonwhite people. Usually when something cannot fit into a white system or does not lend itself easily to analysis, whites arrogantly dismiss it or destroy it. Often times in their attempt to dismiss or destroy, their arrogance gets them killed. The greatest success against whites is experienced when those of us that oppose them resort to tactics that turn the rigid predictable nature of whites against themselves. In many campaigns the most well equipped armies were defeated by opponents that engaged in the unorthodox. Hannibal, the North Vietnamese, the Afghanistan rebels, the Native American, the Africans fighting against European invasion. In many of these instances whites were surprised to find that the forces that opposed them were able to withstand their supposed superiority in weaponry and numbers. In actuality whites were confronted with their own cowardice. The British were picked off during the American Revolution because they were afraid to break ranks and take cover. They believed that their structure and organization would protect them. This may work, but only against tactics that are equally as structured. It was the same case in Vietnam. Guerrilla warfare proved victorious because those that employed it had no reliance or false sense of security based on structure or technology. Whites believe that they can destroy a foe by racking up a high body count and seizing the land and resources of the enemy. They fail to understand that an idea, a cause, and a spirit cannot be killed. Whites have killed over a billion blacks and many of our greatest leaders as a result of their conquests and paranoid protectionism. What they fail to do is kill the idea or the spirit that many of us live by. You cannot beat an enemy that is willing to die for what they believe in, and do anything necessary to gain freedom. Whites will back off respectfully after they have reached the conclusion that their enemy does not fear death, and most certainly has no regard for white life.

Whites constantly fight a battle to submerge their soul. During the Harlem renaissance, whites used to flock to Harlem to be with those soulful black people. Whites could let their hair down without the fear of doing damage to their superior rigid control image. In the recent past you could find them on the Arsenio show pumping their fists and barking in concert with blacks. Before white youths have to assume their pre-defined rigid white control roles, many of them rebel with wild music, drugs, and lewd behavior, all in protest. Many rebel for a short time and eventually accept their constipated conservative role. Others become sucked up in rebellion to the extent that they do not become responsible citizens of any form. Thus, the continued submission of the white man's soul will cause his ultimate implosive self destruction, as well as retard the productivity of the rest of us.

Embodiment

There is a shining example that emerged in the not to distant past that embodies much of what I have said about the white male. If he was forgotten, allow me to resurrect him briefly for discussion's sake. At one time this individual was a living breathing cyst on the almost invisible, cancerous white collective body. This man was only the exposed tip of an iceberg that still runs miles deep. This person is most assuredly a future political figure, The Honorable Mr. David Duke. This man is such a refreshing breath of air, that we Newjacks must inhale deeply to intoxicate ourselves with this dose of white reality. David Duke is the embodiment of the white psyche and persona. He is the classic paranoid white caught up in a drama for survival as evidenced by his allegiance to the KKK. David Duke symbolizes the changing face (with the help of plastic surgery) of the white desire for domination and control. His overt tactics in the KKK were not effective. Therefore he traded in his sheet and hood for a three-piece suit. In this guise he could most effectively exploit the paranoid nature of whites regarding the genetic walls of annihilation that are tumbling down. He was fortunate to come into the public light when white paranoia was at a peak. He came when there wasn't enough money or jobs to go around, and the arrogant nature of whites is looking for somewhere to point the finger of blame. David Duke was good enough to point out that a large portion of the country's problems are due to the welfare system, immigration, and the eroding of white Christian values. This is regardless of the other high level problems caused by white males. Duke's utilization of short-term memory and selective denial was nothing less than masterful. He has written on the subject of the Holocaust and how it never happened, as well as how slavery was a benign efficient economic system. He also naturally utilized propaganda (eternal friend of the white man) to sway the sheepish masses who were searching for something to believe that would make their worthless lives appear to have value. This man was wickedly beautiful! He was the most stunning stand out symbol of the white collective body that anyone could ask for. This man is the embodiment of that which lies at the core of the white male collective conscience.

The behavior of whites, at the time, concerning Duke also deserves close attention. All but the boldest of whites backed away from Duke even those who were directly aligned with him. He was too hot a subject to touch directly without becoming implicated. For those who were secretly aligned with Duke's mission, he served as a pariah to take attention away from individuals engaged in covert Duke-like activities. Some whites were upset with Duke because they felt he was premature, and let the cloak off the dog and pony show a little to early by bringing unwanted public attention to the nature and agenda of white America. Duke was basically an ignorant individual that didn't master the language of politics in order to mask his intentions, and as a result was far too obvious.

Duke is an adversary that Newjacks need not dedicate much energy or time worrying about. The true enemies are those Duke supporters that exercise more tact, subtlety, and wield more power than Duke. One must become sensitized to talk of immigration, quotas, hype over the welfare system, degradation of Christian values and similar issues brought up by whites. These people will make themselves known only if you are listening in the proper manner and context.

Conclusion

Simply stated, these are a sick people. They have more healing to do than black people. The impairment to their healing as well as the source of their sickness is their self-serving arrogance and self-imposed ignorance. As a people, their struggle for survival also contributes to their attitudes and actions. Their arrogance is the result of their own self-digested propaganda. They found it necessary to cover up their tracks and justify their presence after they stole and murdered their barbarous way into history. Their drive to survive is instinctive due to their genetically recessive nature and their minority presence in the world. There is no drive in the animal kingdom stronger than that of survival. For whites this drive has propelled them to the forefront of society with no regard for the byproducts that are the result of their evil evolution. Their maniacal desire to survive will ultimately be the cause of their downfall because this drive leaves a destructive trail marking the seeds that they have sewn for all to see. The white male has no pyramids that exist, socially or physically. All that they have is composed of plastic that is designed to serve a short purpose and be discarded to pollute the environment for centuries to come.

Whites are probably the most stagnant people that have ever existed. Why is it that white racial sickness over time merely changes forms and is never cured or destroyed? It is because the condition of being white never changes. They will forever be hell bent on survival. If you will notice, these people merely change appearances and tactics like a chameleon to map to the current profile of social conscienceness. Today this means being politically correct or slyly racist by using phrases such as "Christian values,""founding principles," and "quota bills." The stagnant condition of white sickness is evident from the continuing measures that must be taken to combat this disease. Implementing legislation, amendments to the constitution, civil rights, affirmative action, anti-discrimination, diversity training, are all efforts to patch the wounds inflicted by whites. It is incredible how whites try to treat these problems as though they are not the originators. Whites only agree to measures that are designed to correct their sickness because we can show them by their own complicated laws that they are sick. They would never determine this by themselves since a patient can no easier diagnose his own disease. I find it ironic that they will occasionally honor us for making civil rights strides, when all we did was defeat them at their own doggish game. It is obvious that these people respect those that have the will and resolve to stand up to them, as it is with any bully.

That which is evidenced today is the biggest clue to their past nature and actions that have not changed up to the present. To really look at white people one must take off the rose-colored glasses and see them for what they truly are, which is what they have always been. If one can get past the travel brochures depicting European countries such as France and England to be the pinnacle of civility and sophistication, one will see Europe for the disunited, backward, polluted continent that it has always been. They have no common language or currency. It is the filthiest place on the planet, where the majority of the worlds' diseases have originated to kill millions around the world. They are just now making strides towards democracy and eliminating the last of their dictatorships. As the attempts at change occur in Europe, the citizens engage in factional fighting, Hitler will never die, and these people will simply never evolve without closely looking in a mirror instead of to a marketing campaign. The countries in Europe that have money are the ones that raped the world (Africa in particular) such as England who boasted of the sun never setting on the British empire. The little wealth that Europe has, it stole because they know no other way. South Africa is a model of past European expansion that represents the rape of a land and people that is still occurring today. The whites of South Africa have digested their own lies for so many generations that I once heard a white South African say in an interview that they are native Africans. This person did not even recognizing that they once migrated as settlers and stole an entire country. America, sadly the most advanced country that originated from Europe, resorted to South African tactics to build itself. It took the whole scale mass murder of the Native American by filthy European diseases and extermination, and the kidnapping of those who built the greatest civilization of all time in Africa. The people who built that civilization and built this country are now considered garbage by the white male, and he wishes that he could sweep them into the same ocean they once crossed to come here.

Whites are still the colonizing thieves that they have always been. Today, popular culture (sports and music in particular) is dominated by blacks that have had their innovation imitated and corrupted by whites. It is the nature of the white male to steal that which they cannot create themselves for lack of soul and humanity. Therefore, whites see to it that they jump on the band wagon and create their own fabricated celebrities modeled after black originators to stake their illegitimate claim to that which they cannot begin to understand. They do this for fear that society will gravitate to a culture that is not mainstream white or possibly reject some aspects of white culture. As a result they must ensure their presence in every cultural venue to demonstrate their universal versatility and inferred superiority. If they become completely frustrated and cannot understand or participate in a particular part of another culture, they will dub it inferior and primitive in an attempt to discredit it. If you can't understand it, or fabricate it, or compete with it, destroy it. This is the way whites have lived in the past, and are still living today.

The privileges that go along with being white are easy to imagine. Can you picture how nice it must be to feel comfortable and welcome in most every environment? To have store owners not fear you, to be seated promptly in restaurants, to get preferential treatment for jobs and bank loans, not having to worry about being hated, or being seen as inferior? Whites are very sensitive to the smallest amount of these advantages being removed. Welfare, affirmative action, equal funding for schools, are all policies that whites dislike because these extremely selfish people are not being directly afforded advantage. White affirmative action has existed forever, and that is the only policy that they want to see continued. For every black person that is afforded an equal and fair opportunity, that is one less white person afforded unfair advantage.

Reality has always denied these people. They found themselves awakening from their dormant condition in Europe to find that the world was on the verge of passing them by. As a result, whites took it upon themselves to carve out their illegitimate niche in a world that had advanced without them. Whites today still are confronted with their inadequacies on a daily basis, from their pale physical appearance, to their inability to play a dominant role in mainstream culture. Their inability will never change since we have established that the beast does not change its stripes, merely its actions. In order to brain wash themselves and other lost souls that lack identity, whites will attempt to highlight certain physical qualities. They make issue of light eyes and blond hair that would otherwise make them appear as genetic mutants in comparison to the composition of the world. Most people in the world have brown or black hair and dark eyes. The appearance of whites is accounted for by having marketing campaigns like the colored contact commercial that addresses such issues as their melanin-deficient blue and green eyes as being desirable. Whites see themselves as being drastically different in appearance compared to most people and must justify this difference and use it as a mechanism for elitism. The reaction that whites have when they are confronted with their differences and inadequacies is an interesting one. It causes whites to strike out in frustrated anger at that which they cannot understand or eliminate. They even will ironically strike out at the people that they desire to be more like, blacks, as is evidenced by their tanning and their gravitation to black culture and beauty. These people's souls are dying to return to that which they came from, but they are caught up in a struggle to maintain their rigid authoritative posture.

Whites are not our gods or masters. They are simply people of flesh and blood that really have no history of accomplishment other than that which was stolen or corrupted. The obstacle that they pose exists only for an unenlightened individual, not a Newjack. The white male is engaged in the mother of all battles at this current time. He is faced with zero population growth in this country, increased immigration, the deteriorating economic position of this nation in the world market, advances being made by minorities and women, the Asians coming on with and ever increasing vengeance, the dynamic theater of operations in Europe, the breakup of Russia, and the impossible task of trying to resolve conflicts among European nations along ethnic, cultural, and economic, lines. High level whites in this country have become so arrogant, fat and complacent, that they are not concerned with pulling their own down trodden white people on the lowest rung of society. "White trash" will always be "white trash." These complex problems and their diverse solutions will never allow whites to be a completely unified people. We must realize that whites are a minority on this planet and there is no way that they can tend to all these issues at the same time.

EON

The reign of white people has been but a mere 400 years at best! We must realize that those ole Africans who built the pyramids ruled the world for **THOUSANDS** of years. We had a dynasty that has not since been duplicated. The reason for this longevity is that the values that our ancestors lived by were built on soul and oneness with the environment with a vision of the future clearly in mind. I submit that the rule of whites will be the shortest rule of any people that were at any time in the forefront of society. This is due to their lack of soul, conscience, and spirit. They are far to hell bent on their immediate survival to be concerned with inner development and long-term vision. We can plainly see evidence today of the failure of white systems that lack humanity and soul because they are designed to simply afford advantage and control, not organization nor harmony. The criminal justice system does not work since it is designed to sweep people under the rug and dehabilitate. Their economic systems don't work, since money itself is designed to make some people rich and other people poor. This is based on the simple fact that if everyone had the same amount of money, what would be its need? Since money is such a driving factor in white society, it has sweeping effects when people cannot afford school, medicine, housing, or food. Since white solutions are always a quick fix, the long-term effect of the policies they implement usually serves to exacerbate the original problem that the policy was intended to solve. Whites lack of soul and feeling leads them to believe that every problem can be fixed with a system that funnels people into predetermined roles. Yet they will never realize that the answer lies in a soul that they do not have. The byproducts of white civilization have literally destroyed the environment and disenfranchised entire peoples based on the color of their skin. However, even with those long term effects, there are plenty of white people content to simply make big money real quick in order to distance themselves and live comfortably far away from the problems they have created. But once again the white man doesn't realize that the destruction created by his wake will one day engulf him. Even his much valued technology that is designed to distance himself from nonwhites, is in contrary fashion holding him more accountable. Remember, the seeds of revolution almost took root in Los Angeles due to the use of a simple camcorder.

Derailment

From the beginning, society was a speeding locomotive on the verge of passing white existence. Whites recognized this fact and acted instinctively out of survival to hijack the train; holding some of its operators and builders captive while others were thrown clear off. Up until the time of its seizure, the train had successfully run on a fuel known as soul and spirituality that burned slowly and remained hot. The train had all that it required to reach its ultimate destination that would empower its passengers to become one with time, space, and God. The hijackers could not understand this fuel that the train utilized, its operation, and most certainly not its destination. Therefore, they created their own fast burning toxic fuel whose byproducts corrupted the environment and put the train on a fast-paced uncharted, undetermined, destination to nowhere. In relation to its rate of speed and the incompetence of its hijackers, this vehicle will either burn up or run into the side of a mountain in the middle of the night. At any rate the train will one day be back in the hands of those who created it and once piloted it. Even if it ends up in 1000 pieces, rebuilding will not be a problem since it was derived from the soul that its creators can never be stripped of.

On Black

My people. Black people. I do indeed love you. You are the original people of the human race. You are the first humans to have ever walked the earth and created the most advanced civilization in Egypt that has ever existed. The likes of which cannot be understood or duplicated today. Besides the obvious architectural achievements, this highly advanced society originated the concepts of spirituality and religion, art, medicine, philosophy, government, math, astronomy and so much more. Less capable and deserving people such as the Greeks felt the need to steal and lay claim to these accomplishments. With such a jewel as this in existence, it is almost understandable how the European barbarians raped all that Africa had to offer including the physical theft of its people. The Europeans wanted only the best to imitate, to rape and to enslave to build their countries. It was only natural that these people gravitate back to Africa from whence they came long ago after their European ice age exile. They came back with a fury. Perhaps we weren't ready to defend the jewel of civilization from the white raiders due to many circumstances both natural and imposed that worked to their advantage. However, that is life. Here we are today in America after a legacy of 400 some odd years of servitude to build this country. Incredibly, African Americans who are the descendants of the mother land, are in the best position to do the most for African peoples everywhere. True we are "free" by the strictest definition of the word. However, we have naturally been made consumers, renters and economic slaves that have been made to believe that we have little power to improve our condition. Like most of the what the white male collective desires us to believe, this is a falsehood. The lack of realization of this lie is the most frustrating aspect of being black. Once one knows our true history, it is difficult to understand how on earth our people could possibly be in the condition that we are presently confronted with. We have been so raped of identity, land and history that we are ourselves lost in a void of self concept and self development.

The problems of black America are numerous yet simple to target because they all rest in one place. The location is within the gray matter between our ears. Once we have a true understanding of ourselves and the forces that attempt to impact us, we can take full responsibility for our condition and actions. The writing of this book is an attempt to increase common understanding so we all know the game that is being run, how we fit in, the problems within our own team, and how we implement strategy to win. I will not fool myself into believing that this document is the answer to even a small portion of our problems. As far as playing the game and understanding the applicable rules, we are not even in a position to find the stadium where the game is taking place, let alone play. Some of us don't even desire to play, some would rather sit in the stands drink beer, boo and cry foul. We have much work to do for those that are willing to accept the challenge of stepping on to the playing field.

EON

History

Some more brief words about history. This book will not attempt to tell of the rich African legacy that our ancestors laid down and almost had destroyed by lesser people. Other books are much better suited to this task and must be read. However with regard to the past, I must state that history is all that black people have to anchor them in this sea of human existence. I have found that those who have no sense of the past are the most pathetic, confused, lost individuals that one could ever come across. Show me a lost black person, and I will bet that individual has no sense of their history. Blacks must identify with the plight of their ancestors to the extent that their pain is our pain. When you read the atrocities that have been committed across the world on a seemingly coordinated scale by whites against blacks, one should not read coldly and without feeling. One should have their heart ripped apart, feel pain and anger, and come to the conclusion that this will happen again only over our dead bodies. This tie to the past must not stop when the book is put away. We should be ever aware that if it were not for time and chance, those of us here today could have been those ole Africans out in the field toiling "fo massa." We must also realize that we were not magically set free because of the goodness in the white male's heart, which in and of itself is an impossibility. We were set free because of the disagreement over the right of states to govern themselves. It was also an economic burden to keep so many tax payers, renters and consumers in captivity with a large maintenance overhead that was not offset by profits. Many blacks like to think of Lincoln as our Messiah, and look to this day for some white male (that will never come) to save us from our pathetic condition. Need I state how long you will be waiting? We must realize that we are still carrying the chains of our ancestors, regardless of how comfortable our individual situations may be. As we walk down the street, we must realize that we could be in chains. When lunch time comes and we say that we are starving, most of us probably don't know the true meaning of the word. As we sit in our air-conditioned offices we must imagine ourselves in the cotton fields. As we complain of our hour long commute in luxury vehicles, we must remember our brothers and sisters in South Africa who walk 15 and 20 miles for water and work each day. We must also realize that most importantly, those of us that are "making it," are everything that those ole Africans ever dreamed of being in their wildest fantasies. We have the responsibility to act accordingly and not dishonor them. Unfortunately, we do not act accordingly.

Why is it that our history is down-played by whites? Naturally the answer is because they have none of their own to compare it to which is embarrassing for a supposed superior people. Also because once you inform a people that they are great, you lose your ability to control them since they begin to think and do for themselves. We must never allow whites to de-emphasize slavery or down-play their role in the extermination and exploitation of black people around the world. We must also remind whites of how this country became a superpower, which was by the expense of black peoples lives for over 400 years. Whites today cringe when their past barbarism is brought up. They wish that it would just all be forgotten and everyone focuses on today, as if their crimes today are any less severe. The average white person has no inkling of the magnitude of the crimes of their people. If one mentions that during slavery and the Middle Passage, white male slavers were responsible for the death of over 135 million plus slaves, a white person enters a state of disbelief as they shrug off the indictment with an uncomfortable smile. It is my hope that the true uncensored story of the barbarism of slavery that occurred during transit from Africa, as well as the atrocities that occurred when our ancestors arrived here, will be told in graphic detail. Perhaps in a motion picture. Naturally this could only be accomplished by a black film studio and production company since we do not have the foothold in Hollywood that other ethnic groups have to promote their causes and tell their history. Other peoples' story, though tragic, pale in comparison to our own. The sheer magnitude of the loss of life and the systematic attempts to destroy the black race make our story truly tragic. The biggest favor that you could do for the white collective and the biggest disservice that you can do yourself is forget your history. Blacks that have forgotten their history or that simply have never been exposed to it, are most susceptible to the same colonization of the mind that whites have continually attempted to perpetrate for hundreds of years. Many African Americans have held on to the doctrines of slavery and accepted their role as powerless victim, just as white America accepted its role as master.

We must realize that our culture and spirit are indestructible, let alone our genetic dominance. Had we been white people and undergone the same plight and physical rape, we would not be present due to a lack of culture and recessive genes. Whites do not realize that you cannot kill a spirit regardless of the number of bodies that are put in jail or piled into graves. If whites ever succeed in killing all of us, they will pay the price of the complete irretrievable loss of their own submerged souls that will be gone forever. We are their only link to their distant past and true spirituality.

Problems Faced Today

I remember President Ronald Reagan asking his audience, "Are you better off today than you were 4 years ago?" He should have directed that question toward our community by asking "Are you better off today than you were 400 years ago?" I shudder to provide an honest answer. When one thinks of the problems faced by blacks today, a feeling of overwhelming powerlessness is almost unavoidable. This powerless attitude, in and of itself, is one of our biggest problems because we do not realize just how powerful we truly are. If we were not a powerful and soulful people, more so than any other group of people, how could you account for the presence of blacks in every field of professional endeavor as well as total domination of popular sports and culture, especially music. This ability is so natural to us that we do not readily recognize it as being an incredible accomplishment for a people that have had seemingly insurmountable obstacles placed in their path. This is coupled by the fact that we are only 12% of the population of this country, and many of our male members are caught up in the criminal justice system. Is it possible to imagine what this country would be like if its entire black population were playing on an unrestricted level playing field where the rules applied to everyone. One group of people recognizes this potential all too clearly, and that is precisely why they attempt to keep blacks powerless.

Black America is the cess pool that white America dumps its emotional garbage into, and the adversity that blacks face is in direct relation to their skin tone. Whites also realize that if they can occupy blacks with the daily quest for food, shelter, clothing and human support, we are in a state of pacification. When these struggles become to much for us to bear they realize that we will turn on one another in order to meet our needs. We also turn to dead end pursuits such as drugs in order to ease the pain of the struggle. Whites realize that painting a distorted picture of blacks in the media and limiting our access to correct these images, will allow portrayal of us in any manner they chose. This provides whites and other groups with a vehicle to define themselves by looking down on blacks. It's kind of like being in a building and looking at the ground to determine which floor you are on. It allows blacks to reach the conclusion that our lives have little significance and our skin color is a liability. It seems that when one is perceived as a criminal, one actually begins to feel and act like a criminal. We experience a degree of paranoia when walking into a shop and feel as though everyone's eyes are trained on us. Naturally the most blatant impact to our person occurs when paranoid white males inflict bodily harm on us, from Emmit Till to Yusef Hawkins, to Rodney King. Oddly enough due partly to the forces that impact us, blacks now live as the Europeans once did, in these caves called inner city projects feeding off of one another in order to survive.

The problems that we, as a people to this day, face are indeed numerous. Some of the most obvious I will attempt to point out. However, we must ask the question: are we partially to blame for our condition? The answer must be a resounding yes. Each of us is responsible for our ultimate destiny. Unfortunately we are so caught up in our daily struggles that we do not have time to analyze the conditions that surround us and take action. We only have time to react to the dynamic conditions that we physically confront on a daily basis. This is why whites think that we complain and beg so much. We are the great emotional reactors that have not demonstrated the ability to focus our reaction to implement change. If something occurs that impacts the black community, our unfocused rage guides us to tear up our own neighborhoods in an irate, irrational display of assertion that serves no purpose. No one in today's American society wants to hear the complaints of someone that gets victimized. The human response is to blame the victim for not avoiding the situation in the first place, or blame the victim for not fighting back and regaining a sense of dignity and respect. It is all a matter of respect, African Americans do not respect one another nor do we command the respect of other peoples. Establishing and gaining a sense of respect for ourselves is the key to our finally carving out a meaningful niche in America and the world. Before any of this can happen we must naturally solve the immediate problems in our community before we venture into other neighborhoods. The thought of solving our problems is not pleasant in relation to the magnitude of the task. However, if we realize that a life of powerless servitude is what hangs in the balance, it provides some incentive to change our condition. What I speak on may seem cruel or frank with regard to my people, but like a stern family member that truly cares about the other members of the family, I will most certainly be harder on my own; even harder than I was on the white folks, if you can believe that.

We Lack Self Concept and Vision to Approach the Future

Our problems primarily rest in the condition of our minds. We have had our slates wiped cleaned of identity, history, self concept and respect for ourselves. We have been convinced by other peoples that we are second class human beings. Humans must establish their identity in order to define themselves and determine a course to follow for the remainder of their lives. We have been robed of this ability. Aside from the crimes committed directly against us, the legacy created by these crimes has caused just as much damage, making the development of positive self concept all the more difficult.

Upon our arrival to this country, we were stripped of our land, culture, dignity, humanity, names, language, religion, and our skin tone made the only issue condemning us to a life of servitude. It is almost inconceivable that any people could survive these degrading conditions and ever accomplish any degree of success in areas not intended for them. Yet we have. Even with our many accomplishments, there still remains those of us that are not enjoying what is considered success in this country. Many of us are caught up in the criminal justice and welfare systems. Others are economic slaves working for minimum wage, renting everything, and are not eligible for any type of assistance because they make to much money even for college loans. For those that are attaining some degree of success, there remains the same factors of discrimination and poor self concept evident in passing conversation when we call each other nigga. When we are asked to identify ourselves, many of us reply with Anglo-Saxon names and state that we are from some U.S. city as our birth place. We do not recognize that we speak the Kings English, that we wear European clothes, and that our demeanor in the work place is dictated by white males. We accept the tenants of this country as our own with regard to its founding white fathers and their stolen Greek principles. In general we accept the attempts made to completely bury every accomplishment of African peoples through the various tactics used to subjugate us. Those that cannot afford education are at the biggest disadvantage in regard to self concept, since they are so caught up in their local battles for survival that a sense of identity becomes a lesser priority. This is why many of the disadvantaged will attempt to associate their identity with worthless items such as cars, jewelry, tennis shoes, jackets, and street prestige. Many poor souls will kill if these few worthless ties to identity are violated or coveted.

Due to poor self concept and the inability to positively define ourselves, the perspective in which blacks put their existence is unavoidably warped. We suffer from a condition that can be deemed *Mind Colonization,* where someone other than ourselves is at the controls. Our minds are so guided by outside forces that we cannot conceive ourselves being ultimately in charge of our own destiny. We act as though there is a need to always look to something or someone greater than ourselves to determine our direction, and we simply cannot cut the ties and dependence on massa. We are so comfortable with a white male as our leader that accepting a black person running for president is more difficult for blacks to accept than it is for whites. We are simply more receptive to white Presidents, James Bond, Superman, and any other white illusion that is offered us. For some time we even had a black soap opera on television playing at the same time as the big white soap operas. Yet it was such a foreign concept for us, that blacks did not support the show and it was eventually canceled. We took discomfort in seeing blacks portrayed in a manner similar to the white people that we truly wished we lived like and looked more like. Such is the damage done by continually and voluntarily exposing our selves to white programming that aids in the perpetual colonization of our minds.

It is difficult to filter out the harmful imagery and low expectations that others have developed for us. Our self concept has been retarded to a condition where we cannot ward off the influences that intend to do us damage. We willingly accept the roles that others have defined for us. We allow people to push us toward vocational training and the military instead of higher education because we have no knowledge of our own potential to achieve. This is related to a lack of knowledge of our history and ourselves as individuals. Whites' ability to influence our sense of self worth and potential is a primary cause of their arrogance and delusion of superiority. Their pervasive European values based on the accumulation of wealth continue to discourage our advancement. They notice that we self destruct when we cannot amass enough wealth to be considered a human being worthy of respect. We have been indoctrinated to equate money with success. In our quest for money we often fall short of our goal of unlimited riches. If we do happen to fall short we either slip into a mode of desperation followed by desperate acts, or fall into hopelessness and despair.

We suffer from our own form of denial. Many of us are unable to accept the fact that we have had a great deal of damage done to our psyches as a result of oppression. This denial takes many destructive forms. The most destructive is the denial of our history and past. This serves to detach us from our roots and dishonor the sacrifices of our ancestors. Many of us love to claim that it is a new day, and lets forget the past and start over with a clean slate. I believe that many of the individuals that subscribe to this belief are quite frankly ashamed of their blackness and history. They fear that their ancestors were weak uncle tomming individuals instead of survivalists that provided hope for future generations. Many of us to this day deny that our everyday actions have nothing to do with oppression and the acceptance of foreign standards. Many of us say that we straighten our hair because it is more manageable. Not because it is a European standard of beauty and we have always been encouraged to comb our hair and alter our appearance. We dream of a European lifestyle identical to the soap opera characters that we admire. In order to take the necessary corrective action to reprogram our mind and its frame of reference, we will first have to admit that we do have a problem that requires immediate attention.

It is amazing to me how fast and consistently we slip into a condition of hopelessness. Our hopelessness is evidenced by the dead-end avenues that we chose to pursue advancement. We believe that success is a high profile lifestyle with plenty of money. We de-emphasize other aspects of development that are based in true substance. Many of us sell our souls for a few dollars and material possessions. We are willing to make great sacrifices of character and dignity in order to improve our bottom line and cash flow. We willingly accept the terms, conditions, and timetables that others have developed to dictate our degree of advancement. By doing this we are the chief instrument of our own oppression and promote the desires of those that would do us damage. We sell ourselves out by yielding to mainstream marketing geared toward the masses. By diluting our true messages based in the black experience and spirituality, we inhibit our progress to the desires and delight of the oppressor. Whites have no desire to subject themselves to meaningful strong black images. This would liberate us as well as educate whites as to our true nature. Whites have no desire for such an education. We sell ourselves short by softening our tone and treading lightly, making sure not to offend. Our first responsibility is to truth and its message of liberation and hope. We must also be willing to accept the responsibility of truth and relieve ourselves of the burden of holding back truths in order to comfort others with a guilty conscience.

We lack understanding of the high level concepts regarding ourselves, our persecutors, their aims, the operation of their world, and how we fit into their agenda. Many of us have not ventured out of our community in body or spirit, nor do we have the desire. Our lack of vision leads us to believe that we exist in a confined environment with no escape. We turn inward in a destructive fashion believing our battles to be internal for lack of understanding the external enemy. Along with the fear of leaving our small worlds because of unfamiliarity, ignorance and fear, we cling to the past like a safety blanket. We do this in a manner that models our slave legacy where we would not make a move without massas' permission and guidance. The white male attempts to convince us that mainstream society has no place for us, and we have no contribution of value. This again relates to the environment that the white male has defined for himself and for ourselves. Many of us suffer from the fear of success and the attention that it brings. We do not want to accept the higher expectations and attention associated with success. We would much rather be anonymous and average. Our children have a terrible sense of mortality because of a lack of vision and hope. We accept the poison introduced into our communities because a quick fix is the only solution to our problems that we have the attention span and vision to accept. The reason that we party like there is no tomorrow is because many of us have resigned ourselves to this falsehood. We believe that being an active participant in life involves looking at six hours of the idiot box and spending what money we have on the movies. This is the extent to which we desire to participate in the world. This would suit a particular group of people just fine since they could control our thinking with imagery from a comfortable remote location and receive all our money in the process. Simply stated, if we do not expand our horizons and realize our role in the grand drama of today's society, we will go the way of the dinosaur.

EON

But We're Victims!

Certainly there are forces that impact us, however if we assume the victim posture, we declare ourselves unfit to change our condition and are absolved of all responsibility to do so. It is the same as someone openly declaring themselves drunk. After doing so this person needs no longer act responsibly, everyone knows that he is drunk, and he has provided himself with an excuse to act an ass. When we declare ourselves victim we have given ourselves permission to riot and act irrationally since we have provided ourselves with an excuse. We are also not obligated to change our condition since we have declined this responsibility by assuming a position of reckless abandon. We afford ourselves an opportunity to strike out blindly at anything in close proximity including ourselves. After we have initiated some self defeating action we will wait on someone to intervene on our behalf. Someone we believe to be greater than ourselves and better suited to improve our condition.

Assuming the victim posture gives us free reign to take part in a variety of activities. We can look and act as we wish. We need not have a clean respectable appearance and can basically treat each other with a great deal of cruelty. After all, we must remember that we are victims and have all the rights and privileges there of. We can act like rats in a cage and feed off one another, or like crabs in a barrel and climb over one another to get to the top. This attitude and its associated actions cannot and will never lead to the liberation of our people.

Are We to Blame?

Should we assume any of the blame for our present condition? Of course, we must. In many instances we can plead ignorance and be set free from blame. However, time and time again we are reminded of the agenda of the oppressor and act surprised when an action such as the Rodney King verdict is handed down, or when a Korean store owner is given probation for murdering a black patron. After we get upset and kill some of our own in blind rage, we again look to our white savior to provide us with a solution. We put them in the position of playing criminal as well as savior, and they aptly change hats to suit our wishes. Whites absolutely disrespect blacks for this ridiculous behavior pattern. Whites visualize us as a dog that continually comes to their house seeking admittance and any table scrap that is offered. Each time that the dog comes to the door, all the white home owner has to do is throw the dog a bone to appease it, and it will go away. Upon the dog's leaving it is also given a swift kick in the ass just for humiliation sake. Whites also know that the dog will be back for the same table scrap and kick in the ass each and every day to follow. Who on earth could respect such a creature?! Those dogs that desire admittance to this house of abuse are looked at as the damn stupidest dogs of all. Thus lie one of our most blatant crimes against ourselves for which we must take full responsibility. Assimilation.

Assimilation

The imagery of the white world and the monetary wealth that it has to offer can be enticing to say the least. Many are willing to sacrifice their identity, character, dignity, and so much more to gain access to even a small portion of this world. The immediate gains can be substantial, however, the long-term cost for what has been deemed "selling out" is far too high. Due to our ability to adapt to any situation or environment, we often find ourselves desiring to give the last possession that no one can take from us unless we volunteer it willingly. That is our souls. In order to fit in and be seemingly accepted, we fool ourselves into believing that the way to survival is through assimilation and absorption. We can be very quick to give up what so many have fought and died for, under the false presumption that we will be accepted as equals. Those that sell out will eventually realize the price involved in sacrificing their identity for that which is foreign and unnatural.

The drive and desire to assimilate is evident in varying degrees in every black person. When we are around whites our language gets a little more proper and we begin to use those words in the crossword puzzles in order to sound more authoritative and intellectual. As if that blah blah language is the yardstick by which intelligence is measured. When we know whites are watching the news and blacks are viewed killing each other we feel some degree of embarrassment. We even feel shame when they air those PBS specials on native African tribes engaged in age old rituals. We seek the acceptance of whites and desire to prove to them that we fit their definition of civility. Civility and the white world are oxymoron's. These actions are crazy and we must realize that the burden of proof does not rest with us. In actuality, the converse is true. Yet and still since whites are at this time winning the game of resource possession and control, we desire to desert our team before the game really gets started. This is under the presumption that we will eventually lose the game anyway. We fall into the trap of associating our value with money in this product-based society, and we spend way beyond our means in an effort to measure up. Ultimately we place a monetary value on our souls in the same way that whites have.

Our strong desire to assimilate is understood by the white collective. They realize that in the instance they fling the doors open to the house, blacks will be waiting to enter like a music concert with money and soul in hand. The strong desire to assimilate has provided for the weakening of our own black institutions. From the Negro Baseball Leagues to our most talented and gifted desiring to attend ivy league schools and work for the fortune 500. We feel that we validate our existence by coexisting with them in their environments. We believe that entrance to white town USA is a sign of arrival or some form of true equality. Why would we seek entrance into any institution that has no understanding of who we are, our history, our struggle, our spirituality, our essence. We were stronger and more united when the white man was overtly brutal and denied us access to his institutions. We were compelled to come together and work with one another. We oddly enough are the first ones to fling the doors open of our own houses to accept whites with open arms, even though they have a history of slamming doors in our faces. This schizophrenic behavior of blacks is again related to our desire to be accepted. We figure that if we open our doors, they will follow suit and open theirs. We have yet to figure that their doors open one way.

Many of us are willing to give it all up, our history, culture, pride, and dignity to join the mainstream. Many of these accommodationists call themselves Americans, not African Americans. They may have skin black as charcoal, yet they make an emphatic point to disassociate themselves from their origins. When one declares themselves purely an American, they fail to understand that they have associated themselves with all the dirt that America has created and perpetuates. All the wars, crimes, murders, thefts and rape. I have heard many of our American brothers and sisters state that they make no point to support black institutions and see no need for the existence of historically black universities and colleges. Many speak against any attempt at coordinated unification of our people and causes geared specifically at our advancement. Many believe that their success and advancement had nothing to do with the sacrifices of their brothers and sisters that gave their lives for all of us during the civil rights era and earlier. Others do not believe in affirmative action and believe that they pulled themselves up solely by their boot straps. Often times they attempt to prove just how objective they are by treating their own people as harshly as whites have. Some even apologize and make allowances for white behavior by stating that problems unique to white people are problems shared by the whole of society. In doing this they attempt to align themselves with the oppressor more closely to gain favor. However, these people fail to understand that whites themselves will use them to further their own white causes. In truth, whites are disgusted by these uncle toms that have so much contempt for their own people. Whites don't trust these traitors to their race and hold them with much less regard than the strong brothers and sisters down for the struggle. Not to name names and point fingers, but I find it odd that many of these "brothers and sisters" just happen to be conservative republicans. Not to cast an aspersion against an entire political party, but I do find it odd. Also these conservatives seem to be getting a lot of air time lately from the mainstream media. They even receive posts on the supreme court. It's almost fashionable for some of us to portray ourselves as contrary to the causes of our community in order to receive notoriety and exposure. In many instances, I see no difference between these individuals and gangster rappers. Both are segments of our community that gain their livelihood from keeping the other segments of the community agitated.

Our ultimate crime of assimilation is in the adoption of the same hate that the oppressor has for us, and directing it at each other. Our calling of each other nigga, sometimes with affection and always with hate, will forever bring us down. Our desire to be as dirty as the oppressor is evident in our desire to migrate from picking tobacco to smoking it, so that we can die just like those that assigned us that chore. Beyond this, our desire to fight the white man's wars in order to ultimately prove ourselves is one of our sickest desires for acceptance. This is not to dishonor those that did their duty above and beyond the call, for what it was worth. However the white male has always had a black lackey to do his bidding who is viewed with more distaste and less respect than those that oppose the white man's dictates with dignity and character.

On a more personal level, some of us will stoop to the incredible level of actually altering our physical features in order to gain acceptance and take part in the image of white beauty. You know who you are; Not to name any names but many of you are quite famous and all of you are at the pinnacle of self hate and brain damage. Others of us born of different ethnic groups mixed with black, claim to be multicultural not believing in labels or accepting our blackness. Basically this group has adopted a middle of the road posture too ashamed to admit that they are black. I prefer that they just blatantly deny their blackness. Many of these people are again in entertainment and oddly enough will sing black, have black music, a black band, all black back-up singers, and will not claim to be part black. Again I prefer that they just deny their blackness definitively instead of playing societal chameleon.

We must realize that we cannot cure our own hurt by adopting the sickness of those that infected us, those who are the most critically ill people on the planet. Our condition is not so hopeless that we need stoop to the lifestyle of the persecutor to better survive. Those that ingest the cancer causing elements of the white world will pay a dear price in terminal illness. Those that get ahead and distance themselves from their brothers and sisters will awake, probably in tougher times, and find themselves alone with the vultures circling. The price of a comfortable life style need not be so high that we sell our souls for that American dream garbage. There is more to this life than a spouse, 2.5 kids, and a house in the suburbs with a two car garage. If this is our only goal, this is all that we will ever achieve. Gaining access to the white man's world should not be the end-all of our goals. We should not act like a pack of happy dogs that have finally gained access to the house so that it provides us with comfort and protection. We should gain access to the house to see how its run, what tools of value are there, and bring those tools back to our own community to be utilized for our own purposes. We must keep one simple fact in mind: The white collective will never fully accept us in their institutions or living with them as true equals, because it would mean their own suicide. These people have fought to legitimize their race from the beginning of *their* discovery of already existent civilization. They will not allow dilution of the exclusivity of whiteness. Whites do not ever envision a world in which they are no longer in control or dominant. Ever.

Cycles of Awareness

One aspect that I will never understand about our people is how we fight the same fight for so long. It seems as though we learn nothing from our past experiences to implement strategy designed for us to progress forward. We have had individuals like Marcus Garvey unite an entire people around the world under one aim in a time that makes today look like paradise. He didn't even have E-mail! Yet this feat has not been done since. It is most frustrating to have certain people enlighten us by showing that the white man's world is all window dressing with no substance, and prove that nation building indeed can be done. We do not take these accomplishments to heart or believe that as individuals we can do the same. We figure that those that have accomplishments are simply better than ourselves and we need not try. Yes, the white male does do a good job at covering up our accomplishments so that we do not get the notion that we are autonomous and can act independently to better our condition. However, this is not an excuse. It almost seems as though our people are simply afraid of success and the responsibility it brings. We would rather have the white man think for us the same way it was done on the plantation. Yet and still we cry freedom. Freedom and having someone else do your thinking is mutually exclusive.

What on earth makes us relax so quickly and adopt a hopeless attitude? It seems as though there is some relation to the weakness of our self concept and the desperate reaction to our situation that we believe to be hopeless. Out of desperation we adopt a quick-fix mentality. If we feel the pain is too much to bear, we do not confide in one another in a supportive environment. We simply pick up a vile of crack, some malt liquor, or go purchase a new pair of sneakers to ease the pain. If we feel insecure about our ability to assert ourselves or feel a sense of powerlessness, we purchase a gun and destroy one another. Our community is the first to adopt any new poison that the white collective desires to introduce to us. He realizes that it will be received with open arms because we are so desperate to ease our pain and gain an immediate sense of empowerment. He also realizes that sufficient aid in the destruction of black people can be best gained by soliciting the help of black people. Our elimination can be accomplished by programming us with imagery of our worthlessness and reinforcing that imagery. Then after these conditions have been orchestrated, exacerbate the situation by introducing these various poison pills to the community. It is masterful in a sick way since we actually look to the white male for some viable solution to our problems. His strategy comes full circle because we reinforce his sense of untouchability and superiority by asking the source of the problem for a solution.

Regardless of the positive that we do, there is this little programmed voice in the back of our minds that tells us that we do not deserve to prosper. And sure enough we meet our, and everybody else's, low expectations. The messages that white society sends are difficult to ignore. We have been convinced that our lives have no meaning and we are a burden to society. There is also a mechanism within us that hears this type of propaganda and accepts its validity. This is the reason that so many young people out on the streets have an unbelievable concept of mortality at such a young age. Many act as though they have nothing to live for by indulging in outward and inner destructive behavior. As much as we desire to empower ourselves, we run from responsibility. With power comes responsibility and we desire the former and shirk the latter. When we act like senseless hoodlums, when we numb ourselves with drugs, when we react to situations violently with little thought given to those being harmed, we have just absolved ourselves of the obligation to act responsibly. When we declare ourselves ignorant, we declare that we are not responsible for our actions. No one holds a drunk man responsible for his actions since it is obvious that he is drunk or has declared himself drunk. I sincerely believe that some of us would much rather declare ourselves hopeless or victims and blame our situation on someone else rather than assume responsibility and the obligation that it brings to improve our own condition. We would rather indulge in diversions like the movies, TV, parties, consuming products, dreaming and dancing than talk responsibility. It is easier and less painful to walk through life in a state of intoxication rather than be sober and deal with reality. Reality is difficult to deal with, and it takes a fully conscious and courageous individual to cope with it. We desire the freedom and independence of intoxication, yet are not willing to accept the responsibility associated with true empowerment.

Black conscience suffers from being caught in a cyclic state of development and never seems to fully mature. When times are tough and the oppressor is most overtly brutal, black conscience is at its height. When the oppressor loosens the reins, tempers the whip, or is undetectable for an instant, we tend to relax our guard and slip back into a state of dormancy. We slip back into our old slavery behavior just like a junkie failing to kick a bad habit. We do not clearly understand that the agenda of the oppressor never sleeps and will never change unless we change it for him. We are very quick to make friends or attempt to make peace, and usually get spat on, gaining nothing, and continuing to lose respect. How many times do you kick a dog before he bites back?

To Damn Competitive and Elitist

We believe our battles to be with each other, since we lack exposure to the outside world and we allow others to define our environment. As a result we are like crabs in a barrel trying to crawl over one another to reach the top. We are in contention for what we believe are scarce resources. To accompany the characteristics of our naturally competitive behavior, we also attempt to distance ourselves from one another by any means at our disposal. We have inherited a very elitist attitude from our oppressor. However, since we don't have our own nigga-like people to look down on in order to determine our status, we seek to position ourselves to look down on those within our own community. We are the trend setters, the consumers, and the people that must be at every party. All of this in an effort to get the attention of the other members of the barrel and "play one another out." We can dub this the *Bigga Nigga Syndrome* where we will utilize flamboyant displays to divide ourselves along the lines of community status and respect. This is the reason that so much emphasis is put on clothes and being cool, running with the in crowd, being "hard," being "down." It is an indicator of poor self esteem and self concept when we must stoop to associating ourselves with meaningless trash in order to determine our self worth and peer ranking. We have given up the notion that our soul and our ability to let it illuminate the surroundings are what makes us special.

The elitist tendencies of the oppressor have had profound effects on our people. We have been taught to discriminate against one another using our skin tone as an issue. Perpetuating this division by the white male has been brilliantly accomplished by allowing lighter-skinned blacks to enjoy advantages in society that darker blacks are prohibited from taking part in. Via this practice, the white male takes advantage of some light-skinned blacks natural desire to advance while creating an atmosphere of mistrust and envy throughout the black community. This is evidenced by promoting and seemingly accepting those blacks that have physically altered their features to appear white. We have bought into this because we love light-skinned blacks, women with long weaves, and nobody put those damn colored contacts in our eye.

The white male can relax somewhat because we have been programmed to the extent that we can create our own divisions. Skin tone and good hair are still issues in our community. We have institutions that are elitist including the church. We have a rift between those of us that have a little money and those of us that don't.

We even perpetuate the insane when one of our own attempts to better themselves. We, like the oppressor, feel that there are limited resources allotted for ourselves. Therefore we have adopted a sacristy mentality of our own where we believe that a step forward for one of us means a step backwards for another of us. We do not encourage those that strive for academic excellence. We say that they "want to be white" and "who do they think they are." We would rather pull them into a sorry condition similar to our own rather than applaud their efforts to improve themselves. If one of us is a nigga, we want all of us to be niggas. This is ultimately selfish and we serve those that would hold us back. When we see someone that may have more success and accomplishments than ourselves, we do not experience pride in one of our own who is achieving. What we feel is resentment and jealousy. We would rather destroy that person than salute and encourage their hard work. Conversely, those of us that are "making it" distance and disassociate ourselves with those elements of the community that have not experienced the success that we have enjoyed. We ask ourselves, "What's their problem, are they stupid?" Many of us do not desire to lend a helping hand to those that we see struggling. We act as though there are a just a few predetermined slots in this world to be filled by successful blacks. We give the oppressor power by believing that our chances will improve if we hold back our brother or sister. We must not be dependent on whites to define us and provide opportunity. There are **no** predetermined slots if we empower ourselves to make our own opportunities. There is room for everyone if we assume responsibility.

Our one-upmanship attitude is also related to our lack of vision and desire to run from responsibility. We cannot determine a coordinated agenda geared toward the future, for our preoccupation with dogging each other and seeking advantage over one another. Many of us would rather reap the immediate rewards and determine some artificial community status rather than be leaders and assume responsibility. We have this simple and selfish need to derive love from admiration, and smug satisfaction from the envy that others display. Many opportunities for true leadership and power pass us by because we cannot see past the immediate gains. We don't gear our actions toward the long term for the benefit of all. A major instance that comes to mind is that of the professional athlete or entertainer that desires to simply sing, dance, dunk a basketball, or make people laugh. Many have said that they simply want to entertain. They claim that they don't want to be leaders or role models. The fact is that it's to much responsibility for them to handle. In an ideal world we could all just do our little job and not worry about real life and the requirements for leadership. Some of these sports and entertainment personalities have the opportunity to be actual power brokers in environments where blacks are under represented. They have a chance to seize power in some of the few venues where we *are* the industry such as sports and entertainment. But we would rather receive the love of the crowd and immediate gratification from small immediate monetary rewards rather than put ourselves in a position to change imagery, provide leadership, and most importantly provide jobs. Today, in light of our present situation, none of us have the luxury of performing our little job with only our immediate concerns as an issue. Today's times require leadership and sacrifice on all levels. If you do not plan to actively participate in our struggle with a vision toward the future and providing direction for those that come after you, please take the next damn vehicle traveling straight to the moon. You would do us the same amount of service there. Coward.

Regardless of the oppression we claim, we are the final perpetrator of the crimes against our own in our community. The white male is pure in his purpose with regard to providing for his desire to survive by allowing our extermination and aiding when possible in the completion of that task. He realizes that he need only supply the combustible materials. He will be removed from full blame by simply allowing us to provide the fire. We have proven that we will literally kill one another to get into a basketball game or party. Who would be seriously worried about or respect any people that would do that. As a result we directly reinforce white supremacy and the notion that we are unable to govern ourselves. Though many conditions are orchestrated, we are the final interpreters and actors in this drama. In spite of what the white male does, he is not entirely to blame since he is an animal obsessed with his immediate survival and destined ultimately for extinction. We are empowered with the ability to change all of this today if we recognize the urgency of the need.

Reinforce White Supremacy

Our actions themselves reinforce this concept. Our past dependence on the white slave master for provision of our food, daily duties, and decisions affecting our lives, in many instances still continues. Some of us, as it was in the past, continue to get our sense of purpose from serving white people like a faithful dog that fetches when told. All creatures need purpose to give their lives definition. The need can be so great that we can often become blind to looking outside of the specific task that is being performed by us to realize its implications or meaning in a broader sense. Many want the simplicity of their job to go unchanged since anything more would mean added responsibility. Quite frankly a primary reason whites do not respect us is because we are not a self-sufficient people like other ethnic groups, and we fight amongst one another for the table scraps thrown to our community by the white community.

There is a certain sickness in putting one's oppressor in a position of power. We are happy when they grant us an audience to discuss the terms for their returning what they have stolen or denied us. There is nothing to discuss! We validate their position of authority over us by entertaining such notions. Discussion with the oppressor also allows them to take part in the process of healing the wounds that they have themselves inflicted in a full-circle drama.

We begin to believe that we are unworthy of freedom for being held captive for so long. We begin to believe that our captor has the right to hold us in captivity. They become our masters and the measure by which we validate and invalidate ourselves. We willingly assist master in breaking our spirit by measuring ourselves by the degree that we cater to master's wishes and demands. We also provide master with feedback as to the success of his claim to ownership of our souls. Positive feedback comes in the form of our hopelessness and inability to take initiative to implement corrective action to improve our condition. When we destroy our own in blind frustration, we assure master that he owns us.

We manifest a certain canine complex as evidenced by our actions. Our people can be so easily satisfied by the most meager of table scraps. We desire to run wild and have a simplistic existence by not directly taking charge of our lives from a position of total control and responsibility. Though we are mistreated, we would rather depend on he who has been mistreating us rather than take the responsibility of fending for ourselves. We lack vision and cannot see ourselves as being self sufficient and independent. As a result we stay close to home and close to that which is most familiar to us. We do not realize that the world is bigger than our own back yard since this yard is all that we have experienced. In many instances we are not as smart as dogs, since dogs will at least go and eat some grass if they know that they have an internal problem. We haven't a clue what to turn toward to cure ourselves. Instead we accept any poison that is inserted into our community without giving side effects so much as a second thought, or discriminating between what's harmful and what's beneficial.

Quite frankly our doggish allegiance to whites in many instances surprises whites. They often wonder just how much they can get away with. They will test those parameters until they get just a loud enough bark out of us to realize that they have gone a bit far. Whites just don't realize that eventually, any dog that is mistreated long enough, will turn on its supposed master. I simply don't know when we will reach that point. The Rodney King incident was very close but even that didn't push us over the edge.

Maintenance of the Slave Relationship

It was a life of brutality and hard work with no thanks whatsoever. People were murdered, families were split up and sold for profit, women were raped, and men were emasculated. We had no control over our lives to the degree that we could effect substantial change to improve our condition. I believe that there must be some psychological term or description for a victim that is exposed to the conditions of their oppressor for an extended period of time. The victim grows to depend on the oppressor in some type of sick relationship in much the same way that a battered wife still loves her abusive husband. Whatever the term is that describes this phenomenon, it most certainly describes our condition.

Perhaps they found the perfect people to be slaves. Our people more than any other, seem to require purpose in our lives. I believe part of the reason that we destroy ourselves is because of a lack of purpose and idle time on our hands. After all, we did not have to build the pyramids. They are not living quarters nor office buildings, we simply displayed creativity, spirituality, and a oneness with environment unique to our people. I believe this strong desire for purpose can lead us blindly into activities with a desire to prove ourselves to those that are not worthy of our deeds.

It seems as though we subscribe to the mad notion that we can one day be accepted if we work hard enough and sacrifice our dignity, character, culture, and spirit. In light of the characteristics of the white conscience, our proving ourselves is not possible. Also, the cost of our very soul is prohibitively high. We seek whites' approval and acceptance at every turn of the corner. We do not want to talk to each other in groups of three or more in the work place since we know that irritates their paranoid condition. We do not want to appear too assertive or show too much initiative for fear that whites will feel threatened. We even feel embarrassed when a prominent black experiences a downfall in the public eye. If one of us steps out of line we have gone so far as to have our entire congressional black caucus atone for the remarks of one individual. As though we all bare the responsibility for the actions of our brother or sister. It is as if we have let down our parents or mentors or other individuals whose approval we seek. Many of us seek to distance ourselves from our brothers and sisters that have fallen out of favor with the white collective for fear of retribution.

I know of one woman who worked for thirty years for a family as a maid and always invited her white employers over during the holidays for many years. She never received a return invitation, but remained loyal and defended the family against anyone who spoke against them. This sick behavior has also manifested itself in other parts of the world where whites have programmed blacks to derive their purpose and self worth from servitude. I recall a South African woman on the news some time ago protesting to whites erecting a fence in their white township so that they would not have to view the poverty of a black shanty some few hundred yards away. The black woman of the black township said that she didn't understand the actions of the whites rising the fence and expressed her love for the whites. Our sick display of this relationship in this country is evident in the taking of the former names of our masters after slavery. Is our good spirit and genteel nature our greatest asset as well as a factor that inhibits our ability to establish respect and true freedom?

There is a lack of resistance on the part of black people to accept the roles that have been defined for us by the white collective. We do not wish to assume the responsibility and take the risk in doing such for ourselves. This is the comfort and shelter that massa has always provided. Like prostitutes in a stable, we allow our white pimp to determine how precisely he wants to use us, and actually grow attached to this relationship as most hookers do. We are also fearful of the consequences that thinking for ourselves might bring about by threatening the authority of our pimps. This relationship is evident in the life styles of working class people as well as those celebrities whom everyone looks up to as being so powerful and independent. Many of us who are "fortunate" enough to have 9-to-5 jobs consider ourselves to have "made it" and look at life through the narrow perspective of always being employed and working for someone else. There is a dear, dear price in accepting this role. It translates into what can be deemed modern day slavery and the sacrifice of personal character to fit into the mold of whoever or whatever is signing the pay checks. We are willing to accept conformity in order to pay the bills and be seemingly accepted as peers with white people. Some of us even believe that we can prove a point by bending over backwards in this type of environment and sacrificing our character. Naturally, we are fooling ourselves. Many modern slaves adhere to the inherent paranoia of their masters by making them comfortable by smiling and laughing at the right time as well as tolerating their ignorance. They want us wagging our tails in submission so that they are assured that we are not showing any signs of independent thought. Many of us are so happy to accept our limited roles that we gain a sense of actually being a part of this white corporate world. Some of us will even wear our corporate badges into those after work happy hours back in "the hood" to show that we have been accepted by the white controlling establishment. Proud to display the brand of our master's plantation. Those of celebrity status with millions of dollars in the bank are, in actually, no better off. A slave with a higher price tag is still but a slave. Many of these individuals are so caught up in their status and salary, that they are satisfied to play a minor role in relation to the scope of their profession. They do not wish to be a producer, an owner or an agent, all of whom are the people that truly have power and make decisions. They are satisfied to live an illusion of power by slam dunking a basketball or spiking a football, rather than assuming true power and responsibility by making decisions. We are satisfied with our roles, from the 9-to-5er to the celebrity. True power and responsibility are unthinkable because of our mind set. We do not realize the scope of the world and the opportunities that exist therein, and instead reject the obligation that we have to control our own destiny.

Assuming Their Standards

We elevate their stature by accepting their standards as the ultimate measure of our worth. Our acceptance of their standard gives them credibility and validity as the yardstick by which we measure ourselves. They also take comfort in knowing that we show no resistance to that which is thrust upon us. In essence we are held captive by our own hand. No one has the right to set standards for all of society since it is composed of many diverse elements. Imposing ones' standards on another can only lead to conflict and oppression. If one accepts the standards of a barbaric caveman, a barbaric caveman is the most that one can ever expect to be. We ourselves will step over one another to be considered a little whiter than the next person. We will degrade our own who might use broken English or who don't behave in a constipated proper white male manner. The standards of the white male are used as a tool of oppression and subjugation. The white man's standards do not apply to him and were never intended to. The white male provides himself with an alternate set of standards that vary depending on the occasion and their application. His standards certainly never serve to discredit him and are used as a tool of exclusion when applied to blacks. The reason that we are told to be twice as good is because we must live to the exact letter of the white man's standards. If we fail to cross a "t" or dot an "i," it will be grounds for denial or dismissal. Thus we have a double standard. Standards are written for all to see and are said to apply to everyone, until it is time to hold everyone accountable. Allowances are made for white males who "may have just made a mistake" or experienced an "oversight." There is no gray area for us. We are required to comply beyond reasonable expectation, and are held back if 100% compliance is not clearly evident. White men need only meet about 60% of what applies to the rest of us.

We judge ourselves by European standards and espouse to live a European lifestyle. We accept their standards to the degree that we judge one another by them. It is beyond me why we would choose to adopt the standards of that which is beneath us and take part in our own destruction. Their programming of our minds through propaganda aids in the commonplace acceptance of their standards. Their images of material wealth, power and success inundate us through the media and entertainment to the degree that we believe them to be the ultimate measure of achievement. Their shallow value system based on money and the material, have made us slaves to our desires and possessions. Long ago they carved out their illegitimate niche in the modern world by setting a monetary standard and raping the resources of the countries that were in possession of the material from which the standard was based. They then turned around and made those counties and their people live by the standards they imposed. We cannot live by standards that were intended to enslave, oppress, and ultimately destroy us. By our unquestioned acceptance of their standards, we have stated that we are unable to develop and live by our own guidelines. We dishonor those that fought and died attempting to work within "the system," to one day provide us with the ability to define ourselves and our own system.

They Will Realize The Error of Their Ways

Some of us actually believe that the President or some other blue-eyed Jesus will come to our rescue. It again must be a behavior pattern of those who have been abused to believe that the abuser will eventually realize the error of his ways and play the role of savior. Abusers must first admit to themselves that they have a problem, and then seek treatment. I have heard no such admission from whites. We yield to the supposed superiority of whites by providing them with the opportunity to cure the world of its ills instead of taking the initiative to implement what is necessary on our own behalf.

Whites' state of denial makes them say with vehemence that "we owe them nothing." Their denial is also perpetuated by their self-digested propaganda that allows them to portray themselves in the guise of dignity and civility. Whites do in actuality know their true nature. The true knowledge of themselves contrasted by their propaganda creates an inner conflict that will one day be their undoing. They will finally realize that they cannot live up to what they have made themselves out to be. Their denial will blind them to the extent that they one day wake up to a new reality, contrary to all that they believe to be true. The revelation of this occurrence will mark the point at which whites will have to decide whether to seek truth, or continue to live a lie and parish. Our community can accelerate this realization by whites, through our achievement and independence both socially and economically.

Black Men

The subject of black men. Lets be frank. When we say the word Nigga, we mean black men. We are the most hated and feared creature on the planet amongst all other creatures and amongst ourselves. The entire situation is ultimately frustrating because self aware black men realize that we are a superior breed of human and the first man to walk the earth. Yet, our current position in this world and the light in which we are seen is contradictory to everything that we know ourselves to be. This is why black men feel trapped due to the inability to assert our superior manhood except through limited outlets. Namely, in athletics, music, and to a much greater extent in destructive behavior directed at one another in the streets.

Black men are feared like no other human being. The intellectual, physical, and sexual threat that black men pose to the controlling white power structure has caused white males to dedicate considerable resources to the continued oppression of our species. Only in this manner can a white male presence be recognizable on this planet with the natural dominant nature of the black male neutralized. As has been stated, much of the fear that the white man experiences is a result of being made aware continuously of their inadequacies, especially physically. And of course we will leave that sexual issue alone in light of how insecure and sensitive they become. At any rate, the realization of their shortcomings is directly responsible for their behavior and their attempts to control and destroy black males. If one ever wants to see fear on the face of a white male, look at the faces of white males when a black man is with a white female. Even if seen together with a white woman during a casual encounter in the office or lunch break. White men feel rage, jealously, and fear since they understand instinctively that any brother with a white female is in a position to physically destroy the white collective. The manifestation of the fear that every white man maintains was evident when four Los Angles police officers tried to kill the image of the black male, in the form of Rodney King, in symbolic yet violent fashion. That same rage and protective instinct is in every white male. Some identify with it, control it, suppress it, while others have no control over it whatsoever.

The efforts of white males have had some detrimental effects on the behavior of black males. Since we are the natural rulers of the world, being placed in a lesser position is contrary to our nature since we have no avenue to assert our manhood. As a result, black males indulge in blind destructive behavior for lack of constructive activity. The rage that exists in black males is probably our greatest commonality. From the most successful to the most down and out, any black male that identifies with the fact the he is a black male, feels the same rage. Whether he questions why the powers that be have done what they have done, or why it is that regardless of education and accomplishment, "you're still a nigga" it's all the same. Rage is OK so long as you do not become blinded by it to the extent that rage is all that you can express. Channeled black male rage as an intellectual motivator could be one of the saving graces of our people.

Quest for Manhood

For men, it is our nature to define our manhood by the degree that we can impose change, and the associated effects of change, on our environment. This natural male desire is inhibited and controlled to the extreme by this constipated white male-dominated society. Black males are continually put in the position where their self-worth is evaluated and dictated by white males. Whether it be our salary, or the decision to employ us in the first place, white males evaluating black males is like a child evaluating their parents. It is a total contradiction of the way things should be. The instinct within black males recognizes this conflict even though we may not acknowledge it in a cognitive sense or be able to articulate it. However, every black male knows "something is wrong with this picture" with regard to our daily lives. The inability of the black male to assert his superior manhood is the root of all black male problems. From the self-hating violence, to irresponsible sex, to drug abuse, to abandoning our women and families, to obsession with material possessions, to hopelessness and despair. It's all a manhood thing.

The avenues for a black male to pursue some sense of manhood is indeed limited. We continually look for a means of expression for this purpose. This is why I mention sports and entertainment to such a large extent. These are avenues that we have targeted to fulfill our quest for assertion that sadly does not go beyond heroics on the playing field. The entire manhood development process for black males has been destroyed and corrupted due to the influence of European values. There are far to many black boys growing up without fathers. Black women, as usual, are doing a fine job with what they have. *However, only a black man can raise a black boy. Period.* As a result, the foreigness of today's environment has helped degrade the process of raising black men. The root of the tree has been cut off, and is not bearing the type of fruit required to nurture and sustain a race of people.

Due to the oppression of the black family structure, black men look for nurturing and support outside of the family in the street. Of course this is entirely the wrong place since it is usually a volatile environment. Black men usually form some type of street support group whether it be a close group of neighborhood homies, or a formal gang. There are few black men who are true loners. In the contentious environment of the street, loners get crushed. In the gang support group, a black male finds love and purpose of warped nature. The pressure to be an assertive man in black society is so great that many black boys have skipped adolescence and gone straight to manhood. This in and of itself is destructive and bypasses many of the necessary steps in the migration to true manhood. At to early an age black adolescents come to the conclusion that their status is dependent on superficial aspects of that which surrounds them. This is not surprising since it is all that they see in the immediate environment and in the media. It's like searching for manhood within the confines of a container that has been formed by society's various pressures and forces over and extended period of time. Unfortunately, this container does not take the shape and substance of a diamond. It is warped, limited in size, and isolated from the rest of the world. Existing in this black manhood container puts naturally aggressive creatures in a small contentious environment. As a result they begin to feed off one another and a general atmosphere of mistrust is born. In the street, black men have defined their own environment with a system of order and social constipation similar to that of white males. One's value is based on street prestige and how "hard" a reputation one possess for either being one not to be messed with or for being a killer. It's based on how much money you possess and how you obtain it, your clothes, car, and how many women (never called that) you have. All of these aspects of street life for a black male are as precious to him as a white man's money and power. All this is evident in the posturing exhibited by black males to flaunt their status to either ward off or challenge other black males.

There are actually two containers that imprison black male development and inhibit their productive participation in family, community and society. The first is the external environment of oppression. The second is the internal self-imposed subcontainer in which each black man exists. The contents of the subcontainer are all that is truly special about black men: their creativity, leadership, vision, fatherhood instincts, love and a passion for life. In order for a black man to expose this side of himself, he must feel secure about the environment in which he exposes these aspects of his character, and to whom he exposes it. This side of the black male is the source of the fire that burns in his belly and is dying to escape. It is also his most vulnerable side. For this reason black men look for an excuse or viable reason to release what is their true essence. Again, I must use sports and entertainment as an opportunity for black men to share themselves without the fear of being hurt. Look at the passion that black men display during sports and entertainment. You will likely only see heterosexual black men hug, kiss, and pat on the but in sports. Look at the passion that the reverend displays when he is in the pulpit. Look at the intense passion of a black man making love. There is nothing like the inner being of the black male which is the center of the universe. We need to work to develop an environment where it can be commonplace to truly express our inner most selves.

I Just Wanna Be a Nigga

I hate to say it, but some of us just want to be niggas. Being a nigga means you can be free. No responsibility. No nothing. Some of my so called educated associates wanna be niggas. Lets face it, being a nigga has a certain amount of attraction to it. Niggas need not aspire to anything, they need not dress accordingly, they need not treat anyone including themselves with respect. They need not earn a living, they need not be educated, they need not take care of anyone or anything, and no one makes any expectations of a nigga. Being a nigga is a type of escapism. You just exist with no obligations. Don't get me wrong, niggas come in all flavors and levels of income and education. There's a whole lot of niggas out there with a lot of money that just want to play political lackey, run a little ball up and down some playing surface, take no leadership roles, squander their money, and die broke. There are a lot of niggas with money that show no loyalty to their own and are even more racist against their own than the oppressor. There are niggas out there that gain some sense of purpose by taking their direction from the oppressor even though they try and act as though they are "down with the cause." There are a whole lot of niggas out there that profess to be religious, but act as though they have never seen the inside of a church. There are a whole lot of niggas out there. To many.

A Basic Level of Self Hate, Rage and Mistrust

My personal rage emanates from various sources. As I look at my brothers and consequently myself, I feel inward directed frustration at black men for the following reasons.

- For our not being fathers
- For being cowards and using guns
- For resigning ourselves to believing that the only way to live and die like a man is in a gang
- For saying that those of us that put value on education and aspire to be successful just want to act white
- For the high value placed on superficial items and equating manhood with those items
- For killing one another
- For falling into the white mans trap (hopelessness, self hate, drugs)
- For attempting to take my son, that has not been conceived, from me and indoctrinate him into your street death culture garbage
- For stepping over one another to establish status and manhood in a childish insecure manner
- For being the main physical element that puts my life at risk every day
- For preferring light skinned women over dark and using them as a status symbol
- For believing that your entire identity originates from superficial European values
- For making money and squandering it on women, drugs, and crap, instead of being entrepreneurs
- For abusing black women because of our own weak self concept
- For not being able to walk through a crowd of you with my woman comfortably

- For the jealousy that you exhibit, instead of pride, when you see one of us doing well through honest means
- For the general level of irresponsibility and hopelessness exhibited on a daily basis
- For promoting empty posturing images to our children and perpetuating irresponsibility and misguided values

It is difficult to acknowledge and articulate the feelings of self destructive rage that I experience as a black man regarding my brothers and myself. If I turn on the television, read the paper, think about yesterday, or walk outside, I will become instantly reacquainted with these feelings of rage and frustration. I cannot escape these feelings no more than I can change my color. With my college degree, corporate work experience and proclaimed self awareness, I still am subject to internal desires of self destruction. Each and every day in some manner, I will be reminded that I am a black man. Weather it be by my own brothers or via some seductive and subtle suggestion by a white person. I think the only black males that have true piece are those that do not identify with their blackness, or those that identify with it but choose to run away from it or deny it. At times I feel as though our self destructive behavior is similar to that of a man that goes on a hunger strike. He hurts only himself, yet and still he gets everyone's attention. And indeed black males do cry for attention and understanding. Though we may never admit it, we feel very much alone, and search for purpose, a venue of assertion, and a place to call home.

We must learn to fight the imagery, the false history, the demons that cause our pain, by identifying and acknowledging their presence, and discontinuing all activities that contribute to their existence. This is a battle that must be waged day by day, internally, until the war is ours. Black men, we must come to the realization that we are the key to our struggle, and assume the responsibility required for leadership. Leadership is one of the most demanding tasks that can be asked of any person. The potential for failure or ridicule is so great that we fear and shy away from this duty. With leadership comes the obligation and burden of acting responsibly every single day without excuse! This quite frankly is to much for weaker individuals to handle and they run from leadership and responsibility by not assuming a sober role in society. Leadership is also a thankless job at times with little glory if you're not in the spot light. Leadership has also proven to be fatal. These and all other aspects that make us desire to be just a nigga must be ignored, and we must step forward without fear. That which was once ours is still there. It is waiting to be reclaimed by those that desire to claim it by becoming responsible leaders, fathers, and business owners.

Women

Black Women. Black pearls of creation. I love you. But this is an equal opportunity book that will leave no one out or play favorites. Our women have problems also, but we will talk about the good stuff first. Of all the hurt that I just spoke of regarding black men, a good black woman at a black man's side is the most special of the few things that makes this world tolerable. The minute I see a beautiful black woman my body functions stop, and for just one second my heart moves into my throat. Black women are the reference point for the standard of beauty that all women must measure themselves against. Of course this is obvious since it is every white boy's dream to be with a black woman, and the skin tone, lips, and figure of the black woman are the objects of envy for every white woman. Now that modern science has made the artificial appearance of the black woman a possibility, many white women are now exercising this option to the delight of themselves, their plastic surgeons, and white men.

Black women have the God given ability to make something incredible out of something that would normally mean harm or destruction. They have beat every odd that has been stacked up against them and continue to achieve. Black women are the givers of life, and I will not attempt to speak on the joy and pain of this experience. Black women have a strength that I simply cannot understand. After the physical rape from white males, abusive relationships, discrimination, and poverty, they continue to survive and strive for excellence. My Grandmother is the strongest person I have ever known.

However, as is the case with black males, black women have also paid a price for their continued survival. Survival means modifying certain behaviors and characteristics of your nature in order to adapt and fit into an environment that you took no part in creating. As a result, black women have had damage done to their psyche to the same degree that black males have experienced. One aspect that is particularly disturbing about black women is their isolationism. Black women have been isolated due to the distance placed between them and black males, due to the environment created for them by white males, and due to their general mistrust and petty behavior toward one another. The independent nature of black women might make it seem as though black women have no companion. This is not true. There is another level of cohesiveness that women enjoy. Women by nature do not trust one another, however they share a collective state of mind that I shall call the Sisterhood. The Sisterhood is the champion and companion of all black women. The Sisterhood defends against all impulses that intend ill will toward women, especially men. There are certain rallying cries that bring the Sisterhood together into a cohesive unit very rapidly. The Sisterhood is like a metaphysical entity that can be summoned to the defense of womanhood with the proper stimulus. The main stimulus for evoking the Sisterhood is any mention of men or subjects dealing with male behavior toward women. Especially if a woman has been done wrong or is in an emotional state of distress. Women have all had common experiences with regard to their interaction with men and in this respect women can identify with one another. The Sisterhood is the opportunity for women to champion their own causes since black women in particular have no defenders or vigilantes to protect their honor as do white women. This makes black women the most isolated of all females.

There are some problems with the Sisterhood. Often it will automatically indict any person that allegedly violates a woman or women in general. Once the Sisterhood has been convened, it does not necessarily act in the most rational of manners, and will seek the opportunity to exercise its influence. It will not listen to all the evidence before a guilty verdict is handed down. This is due to women having been oppressed for so long, that any opportunity to exercise any degree of assertion as a coordinated body is taken when it presents itself. The Sisterhood is very defensive and would rather set a tone that commands the respect/fear of others than necessarily worry about being technically correct in its actions. The Sisterhood does experience in-fighting, however this takes place behind closed doors, and is usually the result of petty points of contention amongst its members.

At times the Sisterhood can work itself into a nationalistic frenzy that leads to isolation. The Sisterhood at times applauds black female independence to the point that it challenges the need for the traditional family with a male in the house. At times the Sisterhood borders on galvanizing hate and loathing at black men and perpetuating negative imagery of black men. This is extremely destructive for sisters that are raising black boys where this negative attitude and imagery destroys the self concept of young black males. Some members of the sisterhood can be so anti-black male that they will not give any brother the time of day. They date, marry, and socialize only outside of their race. This related to the fact that everyone wants parity with white men. White women want parity with white men, black women want parity with white women, and no one wants parity with black men. I think that the women who subscribe to these sentiments are defeated and have voluntarily walked down the path of self destruction. The union and relationship between black women and men is meant to be a partnership, not a competition.

There are most certainly penalties for any black women that violates the tenants of the Sisterhood that could lead to the ultimate condition of isolation. For instance, not long ago Shaharazad Ali wrote a book that was designed to inform the black man about the inner most behaviors and views of the black woman. This was a no no since it was a broadside attack against the Sisterhood that channeled information directly to black men. Black men are not necessarily the enemy, but we are not endeared to the degree of being privy to this type of information. I'm not speaking as to the validity of the content of Ms. Ali's book, however the mere act of giving away what she considered to be the most valuable of women's secrets was considered betrayal. These secrets being, mystery, secrecy, and communication by suggestion, inference and emotion. The sisterhood is the undying companion of black women, but its system of justice is Mafioso style.

Self Esteem/Hate and Assertion

Black women suffer from the same type of self-hate and low self-esteem that plagues black men. However, their self destructive behavior manifests itself differently. Black women have been told by society for centuries that they have no value. They have been used as breeding stock and belly warmers since the days of slavery, and are still not on equal footing with others regarding respect and opportunity. Black women are continually bombarded with these messages and will sometimes display the ill effects of this continuous oppression. Black women realize that they work harder than anyone else to make ends meet, and still they are unappreciated and mistreated. As a result, they suffer from poor self-esteem. They will sometimes succumb to these societal messages by convincing themselves that they have no value and as a result fall into hopelessness. Nothing could be farther from the truth. Due to low self-esteem, black women will exhibit self destructive behaviors. They will stay in abusive relationships because they assume that fault rests with them. They also place to much value on their femininity to define their self esteem and self concept. The emphasis placed on the illusion of beauty is a trap that women are pushed into by societies' pressures. Men create this environment for women and funnel them into it via subtle suggestion and overt overture. Many times women will cave in under this pressure rather than pursue other avenues of finding true purpose in their lives.

Black women will turn to false vehicles of assertion and power just as black men do. Women are the marketing victims of life because the companies that gear their campaigns toward women are fully aware of their mind set. Each time an avid shopping women goes out, she hopes to find a self esteem pick-me-up in the form of the latest fashion wears. With each new outfit she is purchasing a new attitude to be worn for at least one special occasion. This illusion also leads women to believe that the only power that they will ever have is from their femininity and the ability to assert it over men. Many times when women need a self esteem pick me up as well as an illusion of power, they will take those new outfits, their fresh hairdos, and that alluring makeup out for a night on the town. Some women generally do go to have fun, however others go out only to have men approach them, buy them drinks, and tell them how beautiful they are. They wear those pumps like two six shooters. At the end of the evening they will go home feeling good from having their head inflated, but wake up the following morning feeling as any junkie would coming down from an artificial high.

It is also obvious that women are extremely insecure about their femininity and the power that it brings leaving them with advancing age. Why is it that you can never tell a woman enough times how beautiful they are? It is because they are insecure about their power and influence over men fading. That's when they really hit those night clubs for affirmation of their value. This type of value based on physical appearance is most evident in shallow women that have nothing else going for them. Many women would rather have a man complement them on their outfit and hair rather than have a man take a deeper interest in them as a human being. Physically beautiful women also have a curse on them because they are constantly pressured by men, and other women are jealous of their beauty.

Black women are most certainly degraded more than white women. However, white women are also quite sick with regard to the emphasis placed on appearance. As is the case with black women, the white woman's environment has been created for them by white males. White males also place an impossible burden on white women since they must live up to the standards of beauty set by black women. The lengths that white women will go to imitate black women is unbelievable. They will literally flirt with death with these artificial implants, bombard themselves with ultra violet light, and this collagen injection thing I will never understand. The meaningless value placed on appearance is most certainly from a European value system that has infected black women in the same manner that the plague of European values has affected our community.

Are Men to Blame?

Of course they are. White men are responsible for the environment created for women and the value placed on a their femininity. In this respect, black women fall into the same trap that black men have fallen into. Namely, being products of their environment. Men have created an environment for women where they desire them to be housewives, models, centerfolds, call girls, and playthings. Men have socialized women to the point where they feel obligated to create larger than life images and spend countless recurring sums of money maintaining that fleeting illusion. Men don't even want women who are unattractive to anchor the news or be airline stewardesses. Men who have determined that women are a problem must be held accountable for the monsters that they have created and perpetuate. Men must humanize women and take them off of that doll pedestal so they can be dealt with as human beings. If women allow men to determine their place in society they will forever be cheerleaders on the playing field of life. Women must realize that they are in ultimate control of their destinies and will receive the respect that they command.

Are Women to Blame?

Of course they are. We all must take some responsibility for our condition. In some respects women are to blame for the manner in which they are treated by men. Women that say that all men are dogs and that there are no good men left, are partially responsible for this situation. Some women tend to measure many men against ridicules standards and requirements. I know of women that judge men by their jobs, money, shoes, watches, clothing, skin tone, hair texture, shape, and in particular, height. Women also gage us against the images and fantasies that they have developed for themselves regarding the ideal mate. Denzel usually comes to mind. Not to take anything from the bother, but most of us just don't look like that. Part of the reason that women find Denzel so attractive is because he is such a devoted husband, but we won't talk about that female sickness that attracts them to men that are taken. It seems to evoke certain sensitivities. Also, women are to blame for the creation of the gigolos and dogs that meet their rigorous requirements. Women create these dogs because they supply the demand. As a result there are only a few qualified Denzel-like men that have their hands full meeting the needs of so many women. Some women say that there are not enough men to go around because they exclusively demand these fantasy men. In actuality there are not enough Denzels.

What They Really Want

Women truly desire to be assertive and valued beyond their beauty. It is every woman's dream to be attractive as well as respected. I know that I will get into trouble for this next statement however I think it to be true. *I believe that it is every woman's desire to be assertive as well as attractive, and be respected for their character and accomplishments. However, I feel that it is also in a woman's nature to be submissive to a man with regard to interpersonal relationships, and every woman wants a man that respects her, and a man that she can take comfort in submitting to without fear of harm or mistreatment during intimacy.*

Our Children

This is the most frightening, tragic, and depressing aspect of our community. Due to the problems being experienced by adults and the need to cope with the challenges of everyday life, there is little time left for our children. This is evident in this generation of kids who are without hope or dreams, and feel abandoned with no sign of rescue in sight. Unfortunately, advances in technology can make us lazy and this generation of kids has been raised by TV, music and the movies. Children are like anything that has to be grown and cultivated. You will harvest precisely what you have sown, and the early years of development are the most fragile and critical. The world of our young people is pure violence and sex because these are the only outlets that they have been exposed to as a means of assertion and expression. Children are very sharp.

However they will seize the first opportunity given them to act irresponsibly. That's just what kids do. They test the parameters of right and wrong continuously as they embark on the journey to determine their role in society. If these boundaries are not made clear by parents and other adults, it is only natural that the child will go astray like a runaway train. The onus of impressing the need for responsibility and acceptable behavior on children as they develop rests with parents and all adults.

If you look at our children, they live in a very violent, fast paced world with numerous sources of information coming at them from every direction. Without the proper programming and filtering, the fastest of today's super computers would be overwhelmed. It is the job of parents to guide their children though this ocean of messages and signals that preach mediocrity and irresponsibility. Hollywood and the powers that be are most certainly in control of today's lost generation that inevitably turns to the wrong source for answers to difficult questions. Hollywood recognizes the desire for children to turn to irresponsible behavior as an outlet, and will target market these aspects of entertainment in order to make a fast buck. Hollywood does not realize the long term effects that they are fostering for want of immediate reward. The seeds that they plant will eventually affect Hollywood itself.

Children also suffer a great disadvantage by not seeing the type of bold leadership that they should from those that they look up to. When you have your sports heroes allegedly raping women, gambling away fortunes, stating that they do not desire to do anything other than run up and down a field with a ball in their hand; when you have irresponsible gangster rap as the number one seller which preaches treating men and women like dirt and getting high as acceptable behavior; when the true heroes who are hard working, every day, responsible, people become invisible and inaccessible to kids, you are going to raise a generation of human garbage. You can see it in the behavior of our children in the streets. Some troubled kids today dress like trash, act like trash, have little self respect, and no respect for others. The Hollywood values of money and power are what they espouse to, yet they act out of frustration when the real world does not allow them to easily attain these riches. They soon discover that if you are not an entertainer or athlete, it takes hard work, many years of school, a lot of support, and a little luck brought about by preparation meeting opportunity in order to be successful. Kids that have not been exposed to work ethics and the value of time and effort, will lose hope quickly when they are met with adversity. As a result they become frustrated, angry, and begin to look for means to take out their aggression. I have heard some kids say that they are willing to do anything to make money. Whether that be selling drugs, selling their bodies, or preaching hate and self destruction. These children are attracted to these dead-end pursuits because they are not in touch with themselves and have no guidance along the path of self discovery. They have simply not been nurtured in an environment where they have the opportunity to find out what makes them special as an individual. They have not had the opportunity to cultivate this talent into a productive life and career with purpose. As a result they sell out for whatever someone is willing to pay them regardless of how self destructive the activity may be.

Our children simply feel betrayed. It is said that this current generation will not enjoy a lifestyle equivalent or better than their parents. This is because their parents sold them out. The baby boomers are simply greedy people. This is evidenced by the economic upheaval of the eighties and the price to be paid in the nineties and beyond. Kids today cry out for help through their self destructive behavior. Their actions are intended to draw attention to themselves and affirm to their parents that they did a lousy job raising them. Kids say in disgust "look at what you created." "Look at the results of ignoring me in order to get your career off the ground." "I am a mess and I am going to do as much harm to this society and myself as I possibly can." Our kids today end each sentence with a question, "You know what I'm sayin?" This is because they do not know what they're saying, and hope that someone other than themselves can tell them what they mean. They are also checking to see if any one is listening.

The answer to all of these problems is of course obvious and simple. It begins with parents showing the type of leadership and parenting that requires consistent effort and time invested. Most importantly parents must lead by example and demonstrate to the child that is not blessed with a voice like a nightingale or 6'7" 280 lb. stature, that there is another rewarding way to affirm one's value in this world. Parents must communicate that the greatest challenge that faces our people is not making a few millionaires on the playing field or stage, but making a few billionaires that run international conglomerates and provide economic security for our people. Only these billionaires will provide for our people and gain the respect of the world for our entire race.

Our Music

We are music. All music. They try to make us believe that they created rock & roll, jazz, rhythm and blues, soul, rap, etc. That is again because they have no accomplishments comparable to ours. Our music is beautiful and showcases our spirit. Our music has always been used as a means of expression. Some of today's popular music, rap in particular, expresses frustration through self destruction, through irresponsibility, through male posturing and female assertion. Of course all rap is not bad. I was in high school when today's rap craze started. I've seen it all. Today's rap is shockingly violent with its hard core messages as compared to the lighter messages indicative of raps' roots. This hard, street attitude is the undercurrent that the majority of today's rap artists are riding. Even rap artists that were praised for preaching positivity have strapped on combat boots and permanently contorted their faces in that perpetual angry grit which trade marks today's hard core rappers. These artists have most certainly sold out their positive messages for this commercial garbage. Many hard core rappers say that they are just reporters that speak on what they know. If so, they all need to expand their understanding of the world and the plight of our people. They need to stop sounding so hopeless as though they are limited to live the same experiences over and over again in the same 'hood, forever. We need fewer reporters and more individuals that are willing to make the news and define a new reality.

Our musical ability is one of the main aspects of our culture that makes others jealous. It is a pure display of our soul and spirituality that other less adequate peoples continually try to imitate and steal. Through our expression we declare our freedom to do what ever our hearts desire without permission or compromise. Others naturally gravitate to our culture due to the constipated nature of today's society. Our culture provides society with a release so that people can let their hair down. Our music has always scared the oppressor because their children have always gravitated toward it. Our music is a very powerful force that has both a positive side and a negative side. The positive side is a reflection of our soul and inner beauty. The negative side is the commercialization of our self destructive tenancies and outward frustration. The negative side is dangerous since it has elements of the positive that make it seductive. We must deal with the negative side by gaining control of the demons that haunt all of us. It is therapeutic to express our negative experiences through song and rap. But the commercialization of these experiences causes feedback into our subconscious that perpetuates a situation of hopelessness. A wicked cycle of no end that must end.

Church

I, like others who are not afraid to ask difficult questions, most certainly have some problems with the church and religion. For a rational individual, religion makes no sense since it is based on blind faith which is an irrational concept. One either has faith, or one does not. I am also skeptical about religion because of the way in which it has been used to capture the minds of our people and subjugate us into servitude by using the words and rational of the Bible. Before the Europeans brought in cannons, they brought in missionaries. I have problems with the origins of the Bible (King James version) and those English and other European "scholars" that wrote it. Don't get me wrong. I was brought up in a black church and most certainly consider it to have been a valuable experience. I will also see to it that my child has the opportunity to be exposed to this environment at an early stage of development. However, I will not expose my child to a church that is caught in a time warp with a picture of the blond haired, blue eyed Jesus on the wall. It would be just as dangerous to allow my child to be raised by the streets dodging bullets, as it would by this outdated backward thinking. Even if one does not directly believe in all or even some of the teachings of the black church, the black church as an institution of change is indeed valuable to the black community. If this resource is used properly, it could play a major role in determining the future of our race. I have no problems in people believing what they believe, or living the way in which they live. So long as individual rights are respected and we as a people migrate in the proper direction toward a position of empowerment on a global scale.

The church can prove to be a dangerous backward institution where the resources of the community are being tapped with nothing being put back in return. Churches of this nature are peddling spiritual liquor. The focal point of the church is the Minister or Reverend. This individual has the opportunity to effect a great deal of change and be a true community leader if they so chose. Or this individual can be a pimp, drive a Cadillac, have several children born out of wedlock from members of the woman's choir, and eat chicken after Sunday service. The church and its constituents can be a powerful mechanism that can implement change in our communities if adapted to meet today's needs. However, if it is not, it can be as dangerous as any white institution that is designed to tap the resources of the community by providing false hope and no return on investment.

Those who attend church go for a variety of motives and reasons. Most are sincere worshipers who live decent lives and participate in their communities. The reasons that others attend church fall into and out of the realm of sincerity. The first group of church goers I shall call the blind followers. These people are those who simply feel the need to believe in something greater than themselves. Usually they have been indoctrinated into a religious system and have accepted all its tenants without challenge. This group is afraid to ask difficult questions and is leery of those who question their faith. These people have closed their minds to alternative thinking and they live and die by the exact wording of the Bible. This group may not be able to cope with the harsh realities of living in today's society without ducking their heads into the sands of the holy scriptures.

Another group of churchgoers are those who have turned around their lives from a down trodden existence to one of hope. Usually these people have done a great deal of wrong and have accepted the beliefs of the church because they feel it provides retribution for their past improprieties. These people may also simply be unaware of their purpose in this life possibly due to an upbringing that was devoid of proper guidance. These people are afraid to have their faith questioned because it has successfully filled the gapes in their lives. They hang on to their faith like a safety blanket for fear that they will revert back to their misguided ways.

Another group of churchgoers simply loves the spectacle. Its show time. These small minded people come to see who's who, who's with who, how people are dressed, to gossip amongst themselves, be entertained, and socialize. They love to see a good preacher that is a showman. This group really has no interest in religious matters and outside church conduct themselves accordingly until next Sunday. Another group of church goers uses church like any other pain reliever. It is their conscience pill that allows them to get through the rest of their sinning work week. Some of these people need only feel some religion at particular points of the year (Christmas and Easter). They are totally transparent and do themselves a disservice due to their insincerity. Many of this group attend church out of fear because they have read certain parts of the Bible that deal with the day of reckoning. They figure that perhaps retribution on judgment day will not be so harsh if they attend church every once and a while.

Yet another group of church goers are those who believe we are living the last days. These people are so filled with the holy ghost, and prepare for the after life with such rigor, that they serve no earthly function because they are so heavenly destined. These folks attempt to convince others that life is no longer worth living, and that one should consume themselves with preparing to meet the Maker. It goes without saying how dangerous these people are, and of how little value they are to a people that require action and bold leadership in the here and now.

The people that I admire in the church are those who have vigorously studied the bible and other religious teachings. They can present their beliefs sincerely because they live precisely what they preach. These people also have the ability to take the teachings of the Bible and dynamically relate them to today's world in a creative manner that conveys a message applicable to the time in which we live. These people are not consumed with preparation for the after life. They are assuming bold leadership postures in their communities, and preach of economic and political empowerment. Many also have put religion in perspective and do not turn the other cheek when dealing with an ugly world that does not reward the weak or confused. Many carry a firearm in the same bedroom dresser that contains their Bible. They are the Newjacks. Find one at a church near you.

The Answer

Is there just one answer to the challenges that present themselves to our community? Of course not since our condition has so many variables that do not stay the same for any period of time. There are, no doubt, a series of solutions that when put together will provide one grand solution. I do not possess this solution set, but like we all should, I will volunteer some possibilities.

The only way out of this is through the effort of both men and women and by the revaluing of the black family. We are a family and community oriented people by nature. Those that chose to destroy and utilize us realized this, and the first item on their agenda of domination and destruction was to segment and destroy our collective being. This is still done today since the prevailing theme of the oppressor is that black life has no value and is not deserving of justice.

It is not a simple matter of people physically living together. There are black people all over the world due to our involuntary scattering. It is truly a matter of rebuilding our collective spirit that has suffered much damage over the years due to oppression and lack of self esteem. The dominant oppressive force in this society no longer, or should I say rarely, engages in overt action. Their key to our destruction is by our own hands. If they can finally convince us to devalue ourselves, then we will be their ultimate instrument of our own destruction. In this manner they will effectively be able to hide behind their state of denial without having their hands physically bloodied. Therefore, we must revalue ourselves.

Don't Make Excuses for Greatness

We are the first and greatest people this world has ever known, who are destined to reclaim our rightful place as its care takers. To many people, our accomplishments seem incredible compared to our current social standing and the way in which we are viewed by other peoples. Every time I become aware of a great accomplishment by our people, whether it be past or present, I feel surprise. "A brother or a sister did that?!" The reason for this reaction is due to our daily struggle for respect and justice, and having given credence to other peoples distorted views of ourselves. We feel surprise when our greatness obviously evidences itself. In a sick manner, it seems as though we enjoy being as mediocre as the oppressor. We seem to down play or ignore our accomplishments in order to gain some type of acceptance with the middle of the road mainstream. We are the greatest producers and creators who have ever existed. Despite all attempts to destroy us, we have survived. On many occasions we have taken their poison and turned it into sustaining nourishment. We need revalue ourselves and simply accept our greatness as a natural fact by making no excuse for our gifts.

We have the God given attribute of an inner being. The reason that we are not oppressors and have no desire to oppress is because we are the original that everyone seeks to imitate. We start every trend that is prevalent in popular culture. We realize this, yet are not cognizant of its implications and power. In essence we are ignorant to what we are doing because our greatness and creativity are so natural that they transcend our ability to realize their uniqueness. How on earth can any group of African people come together in any given location at any given time, and enjoy the same rhythm and spirituality and general vibe? Black is as much a spiritual connection to one another as it is a color.

All we desire is a level playing field. It is amazing what people can make of themselves when their development is not retarded. We need nothing from those that have taken almost everything from us. Just like our brothers and sisters who flew in world wars, kicked ass in Hitler's back yard during the Olympics, trail blazed the west, explored the polar cap, and sat on the supreme court, we need be provided with nothing more than equal opportunity. Our natural ability will guide our path. The evidence of our greatness is

EON

obvious from the jealous and insecure manner in which other
people of the world treat us. The biggest bullies are the most
insecure who maintain a high state of paranoia mixed with fear.
They fear our ability to survive and achieve under impossible
conditions, and the threat of overshadowing their accomplishments
is unbearable for them.

The Other Man

Considerable time has been spent on a topic that deserves attention
to the degree that we are cognizant of its existence and behavior.
Does the white man hold us back? Only to the extent to which we
empower them. If we demystify them and deal with them for what
they are, we can play their games and win. As is every human we
are in ultimate control of our destiny. White men are not the
embodiment of all the forces that challenge us. In fact we ourselves
give them the majority of their power by lending them credibility
and validity. We do this by accepting their standards and
evaluating ourselves by these standards. We do this by continually
striving to reach the ideal European lifestyle as a measure of
success and affirmation. They are literally the most holy ignorant
peoples on the planet, and we are their only key to our destruction.

We have a responsibility regarding these people. We must
compel them to respect us as have other nonwhite people. The
white man respects that which survives independently and has the
ability to govern its own affairs. Respected also are those that can
defend themselves physically and otherwise from exploitation and
servitude. The white man has backed down in the past, but only to
people that demonstrate no regard for taking white life, and who
show no fear at sacrificing their own lives for a cause. These
people are those that the white man seeks peace accords with. By
nature, weaker creatures are singled out for extinction. The strong
exact what they will, the weak yield what they must. It is the way

of things. We must demonstrate ourselves worthy of survival as a people by once again welding the power that has been ordained us by God.

Education

We must become obsessed with this concept in order to take charge of our destiny. This key to liberation is priority number one and will be a continuous non-ending activity even after we believe we have arrived, so that we never go back. We have the responsibility of reeducating our indoctrinated children. Knowledge must be passed down to coming generations in order to make any progress as a unified people. We must expand our horizons in order to take part in the global arena. Many of us are consumed by our immediate needs and our immediate communities. I concede that we must take care of home first, but we must also on occasion step back and look at the larger world wide picture. Especially since our people have been seeded across the globe.

We can never assume the responsibility of governing our own affairs without education. One would never let an individual fly an airplane without the proper training. So as it is with knowing from whence we came, and plotting a course to where we desire to go from our present location.

We must educate ourselves with regard to the poisons of this society so that they can be avoided. The liquor, the drugs, the cigarettes, the violence, the entire European quick-fix mentality. Some of the creations of this poisonous society can be used to cure our community. In particular, finance and technology I believe hold the key to true freedom. These two items are major constituents in the operating system of modern society. If we are not involved in these two arenas we will not be involved in society, and hence, will not fulfill our destiny.

EON

We must educate ourselves in order to create supportive environments. Dealing with the pressures of society can be fatal if the resulting strain and stress are not effectively relieved. We must surround ourselves with good vibes, good music, good food, good company, good and positive information at every given opportunity. Only if we engage in healing periods such as these will we be able to sustain the battle for true independence, freedom, and power.

Cut the BS and Get Up Off It!

Quite frankly, some of us need to get our asses in gear. Many of us will make numerous excuses for not being successful or independent. Yes, there is oppression. However, when we have become truly educated and informed we can no longer claim ignorance, oppression, intoxication, etc. as an excuse for failure. Somehow we subscribe to the sick notion that some work is beneath us. Some of us that don't have two nickels to rub together actually believe that some work is beneath us. We don't like those minimum wage service jobs in particular. We would rather sell drugs than flip burgers. We desire a job similar to those characters that we are exposed to in the movies and similar to that of the high profile people that we idolize. What we don't realize is that the people with the real money are those that we have never heard of, and probably never will hear of. We ask why is it that the Koreans and other ethnic groups own all the stores in our neighborhood? It's because these ethnic groups have seen the opportunity that exists in these stores. Some of them seem to never close. There the ones that we end up going to get something to eat in the wee hours of the morning after we leave the club drunk and hungry. We would never accept working so many hours, especially on the weekend. We also consider these service jobs non-glamorous. Nothing that we can brag about. What we are not willing to accept is the sacrifice and responsibility inherent to entrepreneurship, freedom, and success.

We also need to get over our tendency to relax so quickly and withdraw our advances into a state of retreat until the next crisis. Often times we celebrate to early as though we have won some lasting victory that has elevated us to the pinnacle of achievement. I have yet to see an accomplishment of this broad sweeping magnitude, and doubt that it will come quickly or without significant price.

With being the most gifted people on the planet, we are also the most fun loving. Quite frankly many of us party harder than we work at anything. We watch too much TV, see to many movies, buy clothes and cars that are too expensive, and get caught up in that quest for the ultimate European lifestyle. I am guilty to a certain extent of this myself. I love toys and they provide me with hours of diversion. However, I also realize that they can be gone tomorrow and are not lasting symbols of success or happiness. We must put more serious effort into that which is more substantive and longer lasting. Knowledge and achievement are two things that can never be removed and will last long after any toy is worn out or taken away.

Destruction of Our Leaders

Understand this: each of us is directly responsible for the destruction of our leaders due to our short sightedness. We are so captivated by personalities that we focus on individuals of flesh and blood. We focus on Jesus, not his messages. As long as the powers that be realize that we focus on a single point of potential failure, they will continue to throw us off course by destroying the human beings that we look to for salvation. By elevating our leaders as the key to our salvation, we all share in the guilt of their murder. Until we concentrate on the messages of our leaders and their spirit that can never be destroyed, the oppressor will continue to stock pile bodies. We must listen to our messengers, but focus on their message in order to individually transform a million realities.

We Have Not Leveraged Ourselves to Implement Change

We have not put ourselves in a position to make demands of the government or any other institution or group of individuals. We are the reason that the Haitians are not let into the country. We are the reason that South Africa's slave society was tolerated for so long. We are the reason that our shows such as Arsenio, Roc, Living Color, and South Central, are canceled. We are the reason that we are murdered on a global scale like so much cattle. We are the reason that they want to close our historically black colleges and universities to merge them with white schools. We are the reason that they want to take your black babies away from you and put them into orphanages. We do not exercise our power to protect our interests. We have muzzled the mouths of our leaders and have not allowed them to freely express their views and plans designed to improve our condition because we do not support them. Our leaders answer to the mainstream, not to black America. Their bread is still buttered by master. They cannot offend those individuals and those organizations that comprise their constituents and funding. If our representatives were truly backed by strong economically viable black supporters and businesses, we would have stronger voices to represent us. I don't know who said it, but somehow "people get the government they deserve." Our lack of leverage is also the reason that our schools do not teach our history and a curriculum that reflects our true heritage and culture so that our young ones gain a sense of self. Our economic prosperity coupled with a mind set that provides for our collective need is the lynch pin to our freedom.

Ultimate Responsibility

After our education and liberation, we must assume the ultimate responsibility by claiming nothing less than dominion and power over the earth. To do this we must be responsible. That is response-able. Able to coordinate our efforts to bring about the conclusion and results that we desire and that are geared toward our well being. As it was in the beginning, and as it will be in the future, we shall reclaim what is rightfully ours. We have the responsibility of civilizing this world gone mad with greed, power and destruction. Only a people based in soul, spirituality, and humanity can save it. Perhaps if our ancestors had the coordinated ability to fight the European plague that descended upon the motherland on so many fronts, we would not be in this predicament. However, here we are and we are forced to play the hand that has been dealt us. If ever we leave this earth by who-so-ever's hand, even our own, this planet is finished. Done, never to return again. We are solely and ultimately responsible for the continued existence of humanity.

On America

A merica is the country that many of us live in and have to deal with every day. We must have a firm understanding of this environment and the forces at play within it. Even for those of us that do not live an America, the policies and practices of this country have an affect on every individual in the world. The personal experiences of black people in this country are intimately tied to the humble beginnings of this nation and the measures it took to build itself. The agenda of this country and the policies it implements are representative of its controlling body; not its mainstream population.

The organization and operation of society in America is carried out by its various institutions. Many institutions and the forces that they exert are at play and dictate the way that we live in American society. These institutions are tied to the individuals who founded them, and they operate according to the history and nature of their founders. Naturally the most influential institutions in American society were founded by white males. This is not to say that they have a positive influence on society. There are other smaller institutions in this country that have a great deal of influence. However, the two institutions that have the closest relationship and most influence over smaller institutions and individuals, are corporate America and the American government. Corporate America and the U.S. government affect the lives of every American even if we claim to not be a participant in either. Whether it be the products you purchase or the policy and actions coming from these two institutions, you will experience the effects of their operation. Often these two have teamed up, sometimes one disguised as the other, to implement their agenda of influence and control. Together these partners have waged wars, stolen, and destroyed entire people for their advancement, and continue these actions to this present day. These institutions are shrouded in mystery, politics, exclusion, and privilege.

The attitude and actions of corporations and the government should embody the principles of democracy and free enterprise upon which this nation was founded. However, these institutions do not encompass the attitudes of the majority of Americans, and as a result suffer from a narrow point of view. The governing and economic policies of this country have worked to the advantage of some and the disadvantage of others. The current state of American society and its tolerance for deviant behavior is disturbing. The actions and motives of institutions as well as individuals are reflective of one another. Many of the attitudes and happenings in this country speak to a general degradation of humanity and values. America is in need of a radical restructuring of its institutions and of its priorities to encompass those of us who are nonwhite males and don't share the values of white males.

EON

Corporate AmeriKKKa

Some people can call this place home. They feel accepted and believe that if they work hard enough they will move up to the top. For some it may be true, and I would never crush the dreams of those who truly want to climb that ladder out of determination or delusion. I do realize that corporate America could have worked for me if I so chose to abide by its dictates. However, the price for this acceptance is prohibitively high. I am a true believer in the rights of the individual, free speech, and diversity. Though the corporate environment is changing, it will be some time before these tenants are truly embraced. Several generations of white males will have died and gone to the ever-after before the profile and appearance of corporate America resembles society. For a black person to be accepted in corporate America, further behavior adaptation must take place. As if our current condition is not sufficiently warped. Insecure white males must be made to feel comfortable and at all times in control of the corporate environment. For black men such as myself, this means checking your manhood at the door along with your coat in the morning. Black men cannot act assertive in this environment or they will be labeled menacing, a problem, or unmanageable. Black men cannot run the risk of being caught in so much as a bad mood on a given day. For me the continuation of this type of voluntary sacrifice and exposure would ultimately lead to my destruction, and loss of self concept.

The face that black people have to adopt in corporate America is as shallow and pale as the insincere white faces that we are confronted with on a daily basis. In the same manner that the slave made massa comfortable by dancing, singing, and praising white Jesus, so must we adopt a posture that puts whites at ease in the office. This behavior adaptation makes us uncomfortable talking to one another in groups of three or more and acting too ethnic. Using street language is absolutely forbidden. You literally become obsessed with how you appear to whites and are perceived by whites in every instance. You begin to adopt this subservient meek demeanor. Whites also enjoy and perpetuate this environment. For example, I was sitting at an office luncheon with some five or more black coworkers when a white male, who knew all of us said, "What are you all planning, a take over?" This was a statement of paranoia, intended to impose division and control. Some of us suffer chronic damage from continued exposure to this environment. Many of us get stressed out by walking this daily tightrope suspended above a pit of lions. Some start smoking, abusing their spouses, and engaging in other self destructive activities just to cope. Others become so immersed that they become "company men/women" and accept the environment and its rules of operation. They lose themselves trying to "out-white white people." Eventually each road will lead to a slow, agonizing, and frustrating death regardless of the extent that our incomes increase.

This environment is full of the same social constipation exemplified by the white male, which is no surprise. The demeanor, protocol, and dress are symbolic of captivity. From the business suit (prison uniform), to the neck tie (chain of obedience), to the ID badge (brand of identification), the environment is totally inhibited with little along the lines of personal freedom. Upon your arrival, the company wants to know everything there is to know about you. You are given an employee number and become another of their expendable assets.

The hypocrisy of the environment is disturbing. It runs like a well-choreographed stage play in black and white. White people read their lines, which are between the lines, and black people react to white lines with our behavior modifications. When whites leave this environment to go home for the evening, they altogether leave their scripts at the office. If they see you at the grocery store, not only will they not speak, they literally don't recognize you. You are just another one of *those* people. This adds to the feeling of dehumanization and treatment like a piece of office furniture, used only during working hours. I'll say once again, depending on your line of work this type of white ignorance can take a deadly form. If you happen to be a black undercover police officer or happen to be off duty, it is not unlikely that you may find yourself shot in the back by one of your white coworkers instinctively believing you to be a criminal.

It's Their Frat

We are the ones who seek to gain admittance to the white fraternity and submit ourselves to this treatment willingly. We knowingly give them the power to put a stamp of approval or disapproval upon us. I personally despise being evaluated by someone that I don't relate to or for that matter respect. It causes an internal conflict to be judged by someone who cannot possibly match your humanity or spirituality. It would be a different issue if whites had the ability to judge us after truly desiring to get to know us. However how can they get to know us when they have no desire to be close to us? They evaluate based on their perceptions and whether or not we have made them comfortable by being non threatening.

In many instances this environment divides us by taking the most talented people out of our own community. After law, medical and other post graduate schools, people have so many loans and bills that they will accept the first lucrative offer by some company that waves a fist full of dollars. As long as education is unaffordable, our people will be continually divided. The seductive nature of corporate America depicted by Hollywood also serves as lure. This is where we develop our European values to measure each other by office size, cars, job titles, and company market share.

Once we get into the corporate world we find a different reality. We find that we are not really embraced in the same manner as they embrace their own. For them, they feel comfortable and realize that they have an opportunity to advance within a supportive structure geared toward their acceptance. For us, in order to advance, we must continually prove ourselves and fight for work that is important enough to highlight our skills. It is rare that we are given assignments with a great deal of visibility or degree of challenge. The reason that we have to work twice as hard is because we have to fight for the job, then perform exceptionally on the job itself. Many of us who do not graduate at the top of our class, but show a great deal of potential, are not encouraged to improve our skills or develop further. This is so we may be relegated to performing the low visibility tasks that no one else wants to do. For these people corporate America is not a nurturing environment. Unless you take a great deal of initiative and find someone to take an interest in you, who will provide you with opportunities to grow, your career will go no where.

The foreigness of the environment is also disturbing. The manner in which whites communicate and socialize is annoying at best. You have to listen with seeming interest to their shallow conversations on their Colorado ski trips, their a-rhythmic music, the Seinfeld or Friends show, the black athlete they idolize yet wouldn't invite to dinner, and so on. They actually believe that everyone enjoys what they enjoy, and cannot see outside of themselves to understand a different life style. If they begin to grow comfortable with your presence, they may slip into their after-work behavior. Many times you will catch them in an ignorant moment when they mutter a racist comment. They may not even try to catch themselves after a couple of beers.

We must recognize that many of these institutions are old and will be slow to change. Do not expect any massive cracks in the glass ceiling any time soon. The white male may bend a little to make a gesture toward diversity, however do not expect the old boys network to roll over and die. We will continue to feel the pressure of conformance from the corporate environment due to the nature of those who control its operation. This pressure will not be elevated until we have our own institutions. We will always be foreign objects in white male corporate American culture because deep inside we know our presence there is simply not right.

The Government

The American government is the white man's right arm. In no other environment can the white man do no wrong more so than in the American government. The American government provides white males with a cash cow by funneling tax dollars into their pockets from lucrative defense contracts and S&L bailouts. The founding of this country was by white men, for white men, and continues to embrace white men. A white man can enter government and commit the most heinous crimes without fear of repercussion. Murder, theft, extortion, genocide is justified by the white mans burden to "God and country." We are even forced continually view the pictures of this country's criminal founding fathers on a daily basis as we exchange our small denominations for goods and services. This government was founded on the doctrines and principles of white male violence as celebrated in the national anthem.

This country was built by a European criminal class seeking freedom from oppression, as if they deserved a better environment. What they "discovered" was a peaceful land that already had inhabitants. They proceeded to steal the land from the Native American and murder thousands via war and disease from their decadent filth. They imported unwilling free African labor to build the countries' infrastructure and elevate their own wretched stature. They wrote a constitution that applied only to themselves, though the voice of humanity over time has made amendments. The white male criminal class has typically had internal disputes over the one item that all thieves fight over: money. These disputes have split this nation for a brief period, and has brought the entire earth to the brink of total destruction on several other occasions. It should not be surprising that to this day, this country does not exhibit a moral consciousness. This would be a revelation since this country has no moral foundation. It has obtained everything through theft, war, and slavery. That is the history of its European founders, and the nature of that which they have founded.

The white males controlling the actions of this country use different modes of operation to carry out their agenda. There are the obvious actions of the government, and then there are the virtual hidden actions of the government. The virtual actions of the government are carried out by various instruments ranging from ultra secret federal organizations, the military, organized crime, and foreign governments, etc. These entities have carried out such actions as, lethal human experiments (usually on us), assassinations, drug dealing, overthrowing governments, rigging foreign elections, starting and funding wars, selling arms for hostages, and many other unimaginable crimes. The public behavior of government officials manifests a state of denial, and is an attempt to instill false confidence in government. Occasionally the virtual actions of the government become public knowledge via slip ups, news probes, confessions, etc. When this happens, government officials use plausible deniability and plain amnesia to cover-up their actions rather than be held accountable.

Other more radical elements of society have discovered the government illusion of inclusion and civility can be a vehicle to carry out their hidden agendas. The epitome of this is David Duke and other Duke-like politicians that believe they have found a way to get back to the good old days. Duke with his plastic surgery, business suit, smile, firm handshake, and million dollar funded political machine, received as much 40% of the vote in past primary elections. Other individuals and groups have their agendas met by political lobbying and large contributions to politicians. Politicians are put in office by many of these powerful lobbies and are sustained throughout their tenure by these groups. A great deal of money and perks pass under the table between politicians and lobbyists in the form of money, vacations, promises, and other deals. It is all simply business under the guise of government.

The vehicle that the government provides has allowed white males to take some very disturbing actions and make some very disturbing statements. One of history's monsters, Hitler, justified his actions under the guise of promising all Germans a better way of life and world domination. Still in this day, sentiments of "new world order" are muttered by American politicians. It is an attempt to empower the United States with the justification of playing the world's police officers and passing judgment and policy on foreign countries.

Only through the government could George Bush pardon criminals and give them bonuses as he exited the White House. Only through the government could George Bush and Ronald Reagan escape prosecution for Iran Contra. Only through the government could Richard Nixon still be considered an honored member of the republican party and receive a funeral with full presidential honors, God rest his crooked soul. Only through the government could Oliver North, a convicted felon, seek political office and stand a good chance of being elected. Only through the government could a stage show be orchestrated with the magnitude and drama of the Clarence Thomas hearings, as he sat before a panel of his rich and powerful white male "peers." Only through the government.

As far as blacks are concerned, we cannot play an unwitting participant in government. We may find ourselves doing more harm to our people via government actions than any other activity we engage in. Those of us in the military cannot act like mindless programmed robots when asked to go to foreign lands and kill people of color for money. After they are exterminated we will come home and find the guns pointed at us. The white government vehicle under its guise of democracy cannot go unchecked. Those engaged in its past, present, and previous actions must be held accountable. Government that is left to police itself will operate with impunity to the disadvantage of our people. We must participate, vote, lobby, and see that our agenda is also accommodated.

The American Way

The American Way doesn't necessarily mean the way of hard work and long hours of struggling towards a goal. People that simply find a way to get end results, regardless of the method, are as celebrated as those that put in long hours of honest effort. This country was developed by a European criminal class of people with criminal principles. They stole the land and stole the human resources to build this country. Yet and still, it is the founding white male fathers that are celebrated and given all the credit for the work of laying this country's foundation. This country continues to celebrate its criminal class giving them book and movie deals. The success stories of millionaires, some of whom have gained their fortunes by less than honorable means, are the stories that are celebrated. No one wants to hear about the working class stiff with the good heart who took care of his family. The manner in which this country views success and the measurement there of, is indicative of the characteristics and values of its founders. This country measures everything by a European standard that was developed long ago. The original European rapists that came to the Americas came in search of riches. They murdered millions and stole all that they could to accomplish this task. It is no wonder that these same values have been passed down to today's society. The embracing of these shallow values is perpetuated in the movies and the continued celebration of monetary wealth. The European state of denial will not lend itself to speak on the development of today's society and what extremes were taken to force these values on the rest of the world. The pervasive values of this country state that if you don't have money, you are not worthy of being treated as a human.

EON

America is consumed with immediate, often shallow actions that give only the impression of a lasting solution. The "War on Drugs" and other purely political actions immediately come to mind. America's *fast-food mentality* improves the taste, not the substance or nutrition. America's *head cold remedy mentality* puts over the counter drugs on the market that treat cold symptoms yet do not cure the cold. America does not have the patience or fortitude to invest the time and resources in long term solutions to its many problems.

In America, rather than take better care of ourselves by eating and exercising properly, we chose to numb ourselves with cigarettes, alcohol, and other drugs. We focus on getting through the day, instead of the rest of our lives. When we look at society from a frustrated and powerless perspective, we do not choose to get involved and implement social change. We withdraw to our suburban homes, decide to get a fence put up around our house, and purchase a gun. When we become accustomed to quick fixes and temporary solutions as standard, we may make the mistake of letting that practice slip into critical areas. There are simply some places where shortcuts and sacrifices of quality cannot be tolerated. American goods and services have suffered from shortcuts taken in quality in order to increase profit. The shortsightedness of government and industry has forced America to tear up the environment for immediate need and immediate gain. Instead of implementing a domestic energy policy that considers alternative fuels, we would rather rip up the Alaskan wilderness, drill off shore, and fight wars for fuel. In order to save money today so that adults have more to spend, America decides to cut education. Adults then wonder why our children act as though they have no future. Kids are ready to do drugs, commit suicide, join gangs, and adults ask why. In a few years we will wonder why the work force cannot read and the country is unproductive. We have also relied on the media to raise our children instead of taking time to raise them ourselves. Adults then wonder why kids have no values. We do a lot of vicarious living in this country through the soap operas, athletes, and entertainment personalities. It is no wonder that our reality is distorted.

America threatens to cut welfare because we feel that these people are lazy and unworthy of assistance. We figure that they will be forced to go out and get a job. Of course we don't realize that many of these people are unskilled and no employer will hire them. Naturally their alternative is to turn to crime. Then when they are finally in the criminal justice system, we send them to jail where it costs more to keep them there for a year than it would to pay a years' tuition at an ivy league college. America solves its problems by creating other problems that are less visible yet more costly. These secondary problems may stay out of sight for the short term, but they simply stir, mutate, and become visible again. This country was founded on the principles of slavery and oppression. The legacies of these practices have manifested themselves in today's most urgent problems.

Quite frankly this country reflects the tendencies of the white males that founded it, and of those that still govern its operation. We have spoken on this already, however the pervasive state of denial that white males exhibit, is exemplary of the way this country attempts to run from its problems. The American policy of sweeping issues under the rug only means that additional effort must be expended to smooth over the lumps until people are comfortable walking over them. America is simply not willing to deal with the many problems that it has created from throwing away entire races of people, to poisoning the environment. White males have an inability to look at the harm that they have caused, and especially have an inability to look at themselves as the cause of the problems. Whites wear many masks and hoods in this society so that they are not forced to look at themselves, and so others cannot identify their cowardice. The inhibited behavior of whites is due to the burden of oppression. When the burden becomes to much to deal with, whites may strike out in frustration at society. Rodney King can attest to this.

EON

The Legacy of "Our" Fathers

The condition of America and modern society did not happen by chance or overnight. Many factors went into the equation over time to put this country and this world in its present state. I don't believe that America's migration in its current direction was the result of a conspiracy, or something drawn up in any organized plan. I do, however, believe that it is the result of the innate nature of the "powers that be," who lay claim to the founding of this nation. I believe that if the voice of humanity, civilization, and spirituality does not speak against the many evils of this society, we will depart on a slow backward journey to the filth and decadence of a cave dwelling European existence.

American society deals with reality through denial. We fill ourselves with marketing, drugs, politics, and hide behind professional careers in order to escape the unavoidable truths of our society. The more that we run, the larger our problems become and the more likely they will appear closer to home. We attempt to distance ourselves through technology. We love faxes, E-mail, voice mail and telecommuting. Soon we will be able to do everything from working, banking, shopping and going to the movies, all from home. I don't know if this will all have a positive effect on society, perhaps it will. Perhaps it will serve to alienate people even more and promote the proliferation of more negative imagery and self-destruction. I guess we will see.

It is hard to say where exactly we are headed in America. The events that transpire in this country and the international policy of this country do not encompass the best interest of the majority of its citizens, only a small minority. Many of the events of late give a disturbing indication of the evils and attitudes that lurk beneath a surface illusion of order and civility. Conscious effort is made to cover the true nature of what transpires in our country so that the forces that pull the strings can continue to impose their will.

The political and economic interests of this country engage in certain behaviors to accomplish their aims and neutralize any reaction that the rest of us may have to their actions. Much effort is spent in this country on Political Indirection. PI allows the US to act under the guise of humanity and altruism to accomplish objectives that are aimed at gaining influence politically and economically. One case that comes to mind is the Middle East war where we acted under the auspices of the UN and lending a helping hand to an ally that had been invaded. Without insulting anyone's intelligence, we all know that we were there to protect our oil interests. The concept of sending America's sons and daughters to a foreign land to die, had to be sold to the public. We also had to satisfy our sense of denial for the killing of more people of color.

PI also takes the form of identifying the most viable scape goat. In the case of welfare, it is blacks that are identified as the major recipients. This lie covers the fact that the majority of the recipients are white. However, in order to sell the idea of cutting welfare reform to the American people, an identifiable symbol that put a bad taste in the mouth of white Americans had to be associated with the proposal. The attention that welfare gets also serves to take the light off of the criminal programs that places money in the hands of whites such as the S&L mess, hand gun manufacturing, the drug trade, and other government programs that allow whites to bank tax payer money.

This country simply doesn't focus on substance. We crank out lawyers and bureaucrats, not scientists and engineers. In America we market a sellable product. As long as the packaging is tasteful and attractive, what's inside is irrelevant. We do not even clean up our mistakes with substantive action. When we have the Exxon Valdez oil tanker spill a few million gallons of oil, or have Union Carbide kill 3000 nonwhites, we don't clean up the mess. We put out media PR programs that show foxes and fish frolicking in the wilderness behind a graphic of the company logo. When that makes us comfortable we drop our boycotts and consume the product once again.

EON

When we in America, the most advantaged country in the world, fail to accomplish a goal we do not have the ability to look in the mirror and find fault. We automatically assume that we have covered all our bases and have done everything within our power to achieve our objectives. We almost assume that we are incapable of failure. As a result of failure, we naturally find fault with the rest of the world and cry foul. We find fault with someone else by claiming exclusion to economic markets, unfair competition, and foreign economic factors as the cause of our failure. What comes to mind are American automotive executives traveling to Japan to cry over these issues. All the while waging a negative PR campaign against the Japanese people themselves. This despite the fact that the Japanese have had a quality edge on American cars for many years due to their management style and manufacturing principles. Also ironically coupled by the fact that 40% of Japanese cars are manufactured here in the US. We demand schedules and timetables for the introduction of American auto parts into Japanese markets. We want affirmative action for cars but not people.

When we get a bloody nose we scream murder and launch slander campaigns. Hell, we demanded a formal apology for Pearl Harbor! We even cry during war. When whites don't see themselves getting all the jobs they cry quotas and affirmative action. This country is naturally selfish and narrow minded and quick to point fingers.

The culture of this country makes us comfortable with hiding from our problems and each other by sweeping issues under the rug. Our state of denial forces us to act in cowardly fashion to sweep issues under the rug. However, if we continue to sweep entire people under the rug, it will be our ultimate undoing. America will have two throw away its quick dismissal of people who don't fit the standard white male mold for appearance and demeanor. Americas' differences must be embraced as its most advantageous trait. To do this white males will have to put their insecure egos in check and stop their continual need to create the type of environment that makes them comfortable and puts others at disadvantage. When white male America realizes that America has a cross section of the world in its back yard, it will be more able to capture global markets and be truly competitive. This is coupled by the fact that the inclusion of a broader spectrum of society will mean the economic independence and empowerment of people that have been denied this right for centuries. Only then can America truly grow.

Events of Late

At the time of the writing of this material, there have been four significant societal events that have made their mark on history. Aside from clansmen running for president, white male thieves defrauding the government, the white male face of domestic terrorism rearing its head in Oklahoma, racial attacks in the U.S. and Europe, natural disasters, guns, drugs, and disenfranchised youth, the magnitude of these four events had an immediate effect on everyone. The events were unique in history because of the inclusion of everyone possessing of a television. When I look back at my youth, one day, I will recall these four happenings in vivid detail due to the extensive coverage that was devoted to them by the media. We all had front row seats in this theater. Some of these events left me with mixed emotions and a feeling of discomfort toward our modern society. The events reveal something about our nature, how we view each other, our values, and the lower levels of humanity existent within us that we can instantly resurrect.

The Gulf War

Would someone please state what this war was about. It was about oil, it was about money, it was about global economics, it was about maintaining our American way of life and the status quo.

The last thing it was about was the value of human life. The added benefit of this war was that it came at a very opportune time for America and its then President Bush. It gave the country a much needed big winner and self esteem boost. The war provided something to feel proud of in the midst of recession and catastrophic domestic policy. The war was a diverter of attention from pressing domestic issues. The country had the opportunity to try and make up for disastrous military actions of the recent past taking place in Central America, and primarily Vietnam. The country never had a winning war event to makeup for the tragic loses and the harm done this country as a result of the Vietnam legacy. The gulf war gave us the opportunity for some international vindication as well as the opportunity to shift blame for any potential disasters to the rest of the UN coalition. Most importantly it gave the republican administration validation for a decade of ridiculous arms spending. It gave arms manufacturers the opportunity to showcase their hardware in the upcoming era of defense cutbacks and increased competition for military contracts. It gave US armed forces' leaders the opportunity to display the value of their service branch to the United States in an era of proposed military personnel reductions.

This war gave us great heroes in the form of man and machine. It gave Bush an opportunity to elevate his stature in the upcoming presidential election. Naturally it backfired since the domestic issues that he wanted to divert attention from became to pressing for even a president basking in the glow of a war time victory. This war gave us general Schwarzkopf. It even gave a bother Colin Powell a little play, just a little, not enough to outweigh his white male comrades. It was pure Americana and has naturally lead to lucrative book deals. The war also put domestic and international faith back into US technology that had been eroding for decades. Even though most of the technology used in the war was 20 years old, America was amazed at the skill of our commanders, warriors, and equipment. The enemy was defeated so quickly and handily with minimal US casualties, that our faith was restored in good old American know-how.

However, after affirming all our nationalism by spending millions of dollars to give our troops the welcome that they missed in Vietnam, the war has left a disturbing legacy in the fabric of our nation. The gulf war has lead to the desensitizing of America toward violence. It has also elevated violent policy to becoming a viable alternative to coordinated discussion and diplomacy. All of us witnessed international policy practiced through the laser sight of a combat bomber. Technology itself allowed us to participate in the messy business of war from a location even more comfortable than the cockpit of our combat bombers. This war allowed us to experience a certain drug like seduction derived from the power of annihilating 120,000 lives without sustaining more than the war-time equivalent of a bloody nose. The whole country was just playing one big video game. This war sets a dangerous precedent. American technology provided us with a buffer to the actual horrors of the war taking place on the ground on the other side of the line that was drawn in the sand. As technology and automation advance, we will be able to further distance ourselves from reality. Especially when we can exist in the virtual world of today's modern computers. We embrace these technologies because they have provided us with the ability to distance ourselves from the messy business of humanity. The business of humanity requires that people respect one another, interface with one another, learn about new cultures, reach compromises, and make peace. Technology has provided us with the option of wiping out thousands of lives many, many miles away where the screams cannot be heard, and where the mothers cannot be seen crying. Millions of virtual lives are wiped out each day by our children practicing tomorrow's domestic and foreign policy on their video games.

The war leaves me with a hypocritical feeling that is a result of our American way of life. Even though I despise the loss of life that took place in the conflict that was over money; Even though I believe that America is to blame for the lack of vision to develop an alternative fuel policy. Even though I despise my brothers and sisters going off to another foreign war, to spill their blood in the sand, to fight other people of color. Even though this is yet another conflict orchestrated and instigated by white men in ivory towers who won't see a second of combat action. Even though I feel these things, I am simply not prepared nor able to live life without my automobile and reasonable gas prices. Some of that blood is on my hands, and yours too.

Rodney King

Witness the feeble attempt by insecure white males to symbolically stomp out the existence of black men. The repressed frustration of the white male was clearly displayed on video tape for all to see. What a spectacle. They physically beat him. They moved the trial to a lily white suburb. They slandered his character and animalized him. They showed the video tape enough times to desensitize the public to their acts of barbarism. They showed it in slow motion so that it looked like ballet. They highlighted the fact the Rodney King was less than a model citizen. They then proceeded to insult the intelligence of a country by stating that we didn't see what we saw. All so that they could escape conviction. They were successful.

Not only was Rodney stomped, but so was the spirit of black America. It was meant to be a spirit killer. Something to reaffirm our status as 10th class citizens. And as usual, we played right in to their hands, and did harm to ourselves in an uncontrolled fit of blind rage and self hate. This insult to a human being and a race will take much time and many accomplishments to recover from. This additional smack in the face of black America gave us yet another dose of cold water for those of us foolish enough to believe we were exempt from oppression. This act stated that regardless of your credentials and accomplishments, if you step out of line at the wrong time and place, there is nothing separating you from Rodney King 'cept time and chance. Regardless of how self aware and proud we claim to be, this incident attempted to reinforce our status in the eyes of the world. Not that we must adopt an "I'll show you. I'll show you just how white I can be" attitude, but it just makes for another distracting battle to fight.

OJ

What do I think of OJ Simpson? A great football player, a marginal actor. Nothing more. I express no opinion on his guilt or innocence. I trust the judgment of the ladies and gentlemen of the jury who were there to listen to all the witnesses and weigh all the evidence. They found him innocent. That's the way that the system worked. I feel for the victims and their families.

I don't understand why people think that this trial has widened the racial divide in this country. It was already wide, and I think the trial simply illuminated certain facts and confirmed certain suspicions. Those being:

- Some white people feel that a majority black jury is too stupid to reach a logical decision.
- Some white people are angry that a black person had the means to afford the best possible defense. They are angry that a system oriented toward favoring whites would acquit a black man. It confirms their rationale for holding back the economic advancement of black people.
- White people are indeed quite sensitive to a black man in sexual union with a white woman. Especially a black man with a problem of physical abuse.

- Black people, regardless of their feelings toward OJ, were simply happy to see the system demonstrate its ability to set a black person free regardless innocence or guilt.

The Million Man March

I went. I was glad that I did. To be together with my kind, black men, at peace, in one location was magnificent. The speeches were good and I salute the efforts of the main man who put the event together, Minister Louis Farrakhan. However, I did not go for the speeches. The reason that I went was to enjoy the positive energy of so many black men in one place. A large representation of what comprises the center of the universe was on the Mall that day. Black male energy and spirituality. We were not specifically seeking concessions from the government nor redress of grievances. We simply came to be together with one another on a spiritual level. What I found fascinating was the reaction of America to the idea of so many black men meeting in peace and brotherhood. Of interest I found the following:

- Fat, white men in the government expressing an opinion as to whom should be in attendance.
- The paranoia of white America at the thought of so many black men meeting.
- The attempts to divide our sentiments and emotions along the lines of gender which failed.
- The predominately white U.S. park police, who have stopped me in my car for no reason numerous times, attempting to underplay the success of the event. Sorry boys in blue, but there were one million people there.
- Some blacks in our community that thought it would politically taint them and put them out of favor with "massa."

- Those in our community who did not attend because they were jealous that they did not have the idea first, or the ability to pull off the event successfully.

What I loved most was showing America that we are not all in prison. As well as demonstrating that the oppressors have their work cut out for them if ever they aim to rid the world of us all. I loved the fact that it was the largest and most peaceful gathering that Washington D.C. had ever seen. Most of all I loved the fact that all the reasons that I had previously stated for my ill feelings toward my brothers, were made invalid on that day, October, 16 1995.

Environment

Just what type of place is America? How does one characterize the American environment? I will say that the immediate gains that can be had in this country are offset by the immediate danger and potential risks of living here. With so called freedom, there comes great responsibility. These freedoms lead some Americans to consume over half the world's cocaine. A large portion of American society does not assume responsibility and accountability for their actions. This leads to a lack of respect between individuals and amongst groups of individuals. Unlike the ingredients in a fine recipe, America's people cannot seem to mesh and form a final cohesive product. Our great melting pots' ingredients are composed of oil and water. Only when there is an earthquake, disaster, war or other shakeup, does the country seem to have one common purpose or consistency. After events settle down, the country again separates itself into its disparate elements. America can probably best be characterized by the division and inequalities present in its society. Much effort is wasted in trying to unify these groups through superficial methods. Some feel that we should all unite under the banner of just being Americans and forget any nationalistic tenancies and urges. Many of us are quick to gray ourselves by giving up our origins and culture in order to assimilate into the mainstream. I do not preach this nor do I practice this behavior. I have no desire and don't see the benefit of giving up what makes us as individuals or us as groups of individuals special. The last thing our people need to preach is assimilating into the mainstream. We need to build a nation within a nation as have other powerful groups. The only way that America's many diverse people will ever get along is by the establishment of an atmosphere of mutual respect between groups and individuals. The development and economic independence of each group should not be retarded or curtailed by any other group. However as we know many groups in America act out of fear and insecurity.

Politics, illusion, and negative imagery are the vehicles that allow some groups to wrongly determine the status and advancement of other groups. This type of inequity is the basis of the conflicts that take place in American and ultimately acts to restrain the advancement of the country as a whole. In this country we sadly have the need to define a point of reference to establish our position or status. We must have a group or individual to look down on in order to elevate ourselves. Each of us wants to do a little better than the other guy. Even a little better than our friends. Ultimately we hold ourselves back through these selfish desires because we grow when we help others to grow. When we help others, we also develop relationships that can turn out to be mutually beneficial in the long run. If America continues to be a selfish society we will forever have an underclass, a drug problem, and unemployment problem, a literacy problem, and any other social ill that can be named. If America is to advance, the groups that inhibit society will have to start competing on a fair and level playing field and stop stacking the deck in their favor.

America is a place of tribes and affiliations. You will not make it in this country alone. It is an impossibility. Even for those who say that they have pulled themselves up by there boot straps, there had to be someone that took and interest in them, someone that gave them a break or valuable piece of information, someone that took the opportunity to give a little something back. One's alignment with affiliations in this country is reflective of the individual, and often is the determining factor in one's success. The desire to belong to a supportive group is human nature. The support of family is a core need in the individual and is augmented and sometimes sadly replaced by external affiliations. At times an affiliation outside of our family can destroy our core family function. Whether they be in the form of a corporate job, fraternal affiliation, or street gang, our need for acceptance amongst our peers can become obsessive and ultimately destructive. In this country we live and die by our affiliations. We should choose them wisely and keep family first.

"Give me your tired, your poor, your huddled masses yearning to breathe free." Yeah right. This statement would lead you to believe that America is an accommodating environment. America is no such thing. America is the ultimate venue to test your metal. The "A" in America stands for adversity. If you keep a positive attitude and let no person, no group of persons, deter you from your goals, you will be a success. There are many forks in the road that have tripped up many people and lead them down the path to destruction. To navigate this country you must have guidance and common sense. If you are left alone in America without prior knowledge of the environment or having been raised here, you will most likely meet your maker. You may suffer a spiritual death and go crazy, or you may become a physical casualty. In this country, 23,000 people are murdered with handguns each year, there are 33 suicides a day, so many rapes and robberies a second, 100,000 plus kids going to school with guns, and so on. Many of the homeless started life as regular tax paying citizens. Many are veterans of foreign wars, especially Vietnam. Many just fell on hard times without family or resources to fall back on. Many are mentally disabled. Yet, regardless of any previous good standing, they have joined the ranks of the disinherited due to the lack of accommodation and support existing in the American environment. There are not many institutions that are in a position to help those who have fallen on hard times. That is, except the criminal justice system that will receive you with open arms when you are at your wits end and desperate. Thru this marvelous dehabilitative institution you will be warehoused as inventory and receive three hots and a cot for however many years you are incarcerated. You will eventually be released, depending on the severity of your crime, with a criminal record and a traumatized disposition. You are now unemployable and will continue to circulate in the criminal justice system. America's front line policemen are also victims of the very system that they attest to represent and defend. These individuals are forced to risk their lives every day to recirculate criminals in the system and gather new inductees from the ranks of the disenfranchised. They are told that they are making a difference, however they are simply the broom that another hand is using to sweep away visible problems. The police are used by politicians as an immediate cure for the ills of our increasingly dangerous environment. It feels good when shortsighted Americans hear that there will be more police and jails. The problem of helping people with true time and effort is bypassed by an immediate solution that appeals to the senses. The police are necessary. However they should be an instrument of last resort, protection, and emergency; Not an instrument that addresses paranoia and denial.

For all the freedoms that America boasts of, the pressures of this society are still indicative of its legacy of slavery. The attitude and operation of American society is oriented toward crushing individual spirit and independent thought. If one wants to identify a leader or independent thinking person in this country, they are always identifiable by the arrows in their back. The dominant white male collective works to shape and control the environment by grouping individuals and steering individuals into positions that work to the advantage of the white male collective. This plantation mentality and white man's burden are responsible for crushing the freedoms that nonwhite males seek, and it is this attitude that inhibits the advancement of the whole of American society.

For all its problems, with regard to the rest of the world, America is the testing ground for the society of the future. If it doesn't work here, it is liable to fail in the rest of the world. We know that communism doesn't work because it simply doesn't allow greed to flourish nor personal freedom, and it's essentially a slave society. Perhaps America has freedoms to the point that they are life threatening, and restrictions to the point that it can be inhibiting. However, as we attempt to govern ourselves and work out the kinks associated with this task, perhaps we will ultimately discover some middle ground. If we give up on striving toward peaceful coexistence based in an environment of mutual respect and inclusion, everyone loses.

The Flip Side

There is another side to the posture adopted by America regarding its domestic and international policies. The government and the white men controlling it will do anything it sees fit to achieve its aims and advance its agenda. If this means associating with criminals and engaging in criminal activity, so be it. This country does not enact policy without ulterior motive or the opportunity for deferred gains and political influence. The guise of diplomacy addresses the American state of denial and masks our true intentions. One of this countries states, Hawaii, was annexed, or more accurately stolen, by sugar barons and the U.S. Marines simply for monetary gain. It is important that political illusion continues so that politicians do not have to answer to the American public or the rest of the world when implementing hidden agendas.

The American way of life has a cost associated with it. This burden is placed on its lower class citizens and displaced countries around the world. The very simple principle of equilibrium dictates that for this country to be at peace, other countries must be engaged in war. For this country and a particular class of citizens in this country to be rich, others must be kept poor domestically and internationally. It would be impossible to get foreign labor at cheap prices and bring the goods back to the US to make huge profits if this weren't practiced. At any given time there are at least 20 wars taking place in any part of the world. The United States and other "industrial countries" orchestrate these conditions to maintain their economies and their way of life. It is difficult to trust a government that has in the past perpetrated actions that have put the health, safety, and well being of its citizens in jeopardy. The United States has engaged in experiments ranging from the injecting of black men with the syphilis virus to recently discovering the past experiments injecting people with deadly radiation materials. All just to study the effects on humans. I am scared to think what other studies have been performed and are currently taking place. Some of the doctors that performed these experiments are still alive and practicing. The Center for Disease Control in Atlanta makes me nervous because of government potential for abuse and its location near a major black population. I saw a story on the center not long ago which highlighted the type of diseases that are actually housed in its premises. It made issue of an African virus (whose origins are curiously unknown) that was known to be the most deadly disease on earth. They said that one tiny dose of the disease could destroy an entire city in a very short time. The potential for abuse and destruction is phenomenal. I don't necessarily trust the government to tell its citizens information that is in its best interest. If for instance it was discovered that a popular food or activity was found to be detrimental to health, the government would not necessarily sound the warning bell. If the industry was key to the economy, if it employed a large number of people, or affected the pocket books of influential of affluent white Americans, please believe that public safety would be compromised. Especially if the public engaged in the activity are black Americans. We can call this the *Malt Liquor Syndrome.* America will compromise the well being of its citizens and of other countries that are not of a modern industrial nature, all in the name of preserving the "American way of life."

Foreign Relations

The U.S. aligns itself with countries that have similar interests and who possess significant influence. Countries such as England France, Germany, Israel, all have similar interests and engage in the same type of game to displace the rest of the world to their advantage. The most notorious of these countries is Great Britain. Their history is pure slavery, captivity, and murder. No other people on this earth run from history the way the British do. We have them to thank for the institutionalizing and economic viability of slavery in every form. At one point in time the British empire ruled 1/5 of the land mass of the world and 1/4 of the world's inhabitants were British subjects. This small desolate rock sitting in the ocean named England. This colonizing, imperialistic rapist, stole all that they have, and continue to leverage their influence in their "former" colonies. In my lifetime the British fought a war over some of their stolen territory in the Falkland Islands. The British have slaughtered millions in their past African and Indian conquests. They even have the gaul to name Africa's biggest lake after Queen Victoria. Of course the United States history is intertwined with that of England. We were a former colony that fought for our independence along with others that have gained freedom. We accept the kings English as the standard of communication, our success in this country is determined by how well we speak it. Not long ago the queen of England paid a visit to Washington D.C. All of a sudden inner city neighborhoods were spruced up and our black children taught to curtsy in her presence. It took this pompous bitch's arrival for our community to be worthy of attention. It was infuriating. England maintains possession of the many treasures of ancient Egypt in the famed British museum. Many of the treasures that Britain has raped from its conquests are housed there. What is most disturbing about this England is that they make themselves out to the standard of civility. From the ridiculous white wigs that their judges wear, to their four o'clock tea, to their parliamentary procedures. This country above all others hides behind these guises that manifest their supreme state of denial.

The other major European nations are not much better. France has fought over a great deal of foreign territory with England in its bid for global domination. They still mutter racist references like those spoken by past Prime Minister Edith Cressen who called the Japanese "little red ants" about to colonize Europe. France has other leaders that are trying to evoke white paranoia in an effort to fight a continued rise in immigration. Israel follows suit with its self serving agenda. The Israelis have engaged in as much murder as was necessary to found any other country. One of their leaders Rabbi Meir Kahane, who was murdered in NY, was quoted as saying that "the Arab was a cancer, and one does not coexist with a cancer, you cut it out." The Israelis have nuclear weapons, some of which were sold to South Africa, and a massive military capability. They have been in one war or another with almost every country in that region since they were founded. They even killed their own Prime Minister at the threat that he would make peace with the Arabs.

We know the story on Germany who is fighting its current threat of the second coming of Hitler. German history manifests the general reaction of white Europe regarding changing demographics that threaten the status of whites in Europe. Germany may be the most terminally sick with regard to race compared to the other European nations.

Regardless of this history and legacy of the U.S.'s closest allies, America has no conscious regarding whom it deals with. The business of today is the only matter at hand regardless of effects or consequences. Currently America is courting the former Soviet Union in order to bring this former cold war enemy into the mainstream of countries that dictate the operation of the world. The US has pledged support and billions of dollars in funding toward this effort, naturally to gain favor and future influence. These efforts will have to overcome the legacy of a backward and outdated Russian slave society. A new underclass is also present in Russia and a true handle on its military, with nuclear capability, has not been achieved. They even have their own Hitler in the form of Vladimir Zhirinovsky who was gaining political ground for a while. The effort of transforming communist Russia into a capitalist market economy will take much doing and much US money. With the influence that the United States hopes to have, we can rest assured that our tax dollars will probably be spent on white European Russians before it is ever spent on any domestic problem.

Money

It's all about money in this country. Every war, classification, division and designation. This is truly the American yardstick by which we measure ourselves. It is certainly not an objective or compassionate measurement. It's a cold hard figure. It acts to devalue the truly important aspects of society and places value in people and activities that have little substantive merit. Money is used as a divisive tool and can be effectively employed to enslave people into a stagnant position. When money is given priority over humanity, it becomes a tool of bondage. 2% of the American population control the majority of the wealth. When people are dependent upon others for their shelter, food, and clothing, they are no longer self determined. They are forced to modify their behavior along the guidelines of those that see to their well being. Money can however serve as a tool of equality and objectivity. It is all a matter of placing the proper value on things that are worthy of a simple price tag and not attempting to quantify the freedoms and self determination that are everyone's God given right.

In some respects money can be considered to be all that is evil in our society. However, money is a simple object as is a book or rock. It takes on the properties that we chose to give it, and assumes the power over us that we provide it with. If we worship it as a God, it will take on God-like qualities and power. If we intoxicate ourselves with the obsession of its accumulation, it will provide the effects of a narcotic. If man uses money as a divisive tool it will serve to segment society along predetermined lines of class. Those in the upper class will accumulate wealth, and those in the lower class will be kept dependent and poor. Money by its history is a tool of division and oppression. Its value can be undermined only through humanity.

This country is forced to implement many of its policies simply for economic reasons. Every war has been fought over money in one way or another. The most recent in the Persian Gulf was fought to protect our economic interests and to protect a people in Kuwait who enjoy an average standard of living that only the wealthy in this country enjoy. The Kuwaitis can afford to have others fight their battles since so many countries' way of life and economies are dependent on the resources of the Middle East. Until the U.S. empowers itself with domestic policy, economics will force us to fight more wars and lose more lives.

Economics can be controlled by marketing and smear campaigns. The recent surge in American car sales is largely due to the negative publicity of the Japanese people. They were called the "evil empire,""little red ants," and a host of other names that evoked white paranoia and dehumanized the Japanese. Issue was made of how much real estate and other U.S. institutions were owned by the Japanese. There was an atmosphere created as though an invasion of the U.S. was taking place. When Japan spoke the truth about America growing fat and lazy, Senator Hawlings, upstanding white man that he is, countered by speaking of a mushroom cloud over Japan. He said that the bomb was made by lazy American workers and tested in Japan. It was rally around the flag time to crush those little red ants. We used all these allegations and propaganda to boost the image of American products and leverage trade agreements with Japan. It worked. The atmosphere and paranoia of world war II was resurrected for the sake of saving Americas economy. When it comes to American business we will do anything to secure our money.

Unfortunately, many institutions in this country and throughout the world put a price tag on things that have already been determined priceless by God. A short while ago blacks were a simple economic commodity to be traded and sold on the auction block along with pork bellies and cotton. An economic system had been instituted and we were its unwitting victims. Standards were implemented based on resources that we no longer had control of, and in essence we no longer had control of our destinies. Many of us after our arrival and spending some time here were in a position to purchase our freedom and did so. Not that this made us free, since the economic institutions that put us in bondage didn't belong to us and still don't. Some things money simply cannot buy. Freedom, justice, health care, education, and our very lives to name a few. Many wannabe Gods have created a market for these human rights.

The innate human right of freedom incurs the heaviest economic burden. Fighting threats against our freedom or life style exacts massive economic cost. In this world, they say that "freedom isn't free." We justify our defense spending by this very statement. Justice, education and health also have a high cost associated with them. The degree that people want to protect their freedom, or restrict the freedom of others is dictated by how much money one has. The money that the U.S. allocates to defense allows America its influence and power in the world arena. Everyone knows that America is in a position to backup its foreign policy with sanctions and laser-sight diplomacy if necessary.

The money possessed by the white collective provides for their security and influence in the international and domestic areas. The paranoid feeling of closing walls continues to fuel the institutions that insulate them from the rest of us. Whites are the very builders of the walls that they feel collapsing on themselves. The white psyche would rather spend its money on institutions that close people out and sweep people under the rug, rather than promote an atmosphere of opportunity. This appeal to their paranoia is used in every political campaign. It's odd how they complain of the increasing cost of living and taxes when it costs 3 times as much to keep a person jailed as it does to educate them. There will only be change when it is truly apparent that their narrow perspective is the cause of many of today's modern problems, or when all the jails in the country bust open and there is revolution.

Justice

Whites enjoy their economic ability to manipulate the very institutions that dictate policy to the rest of us. The justice system can be manipulated by those with enough money and influence. Black robes and white justice honor money and provide back doors in the form of light sentences, pardons and various immunities that others cannot claim. It is a shame that individuals with good character are not given equal treatment perhaps for the simple fact that they cannot afford the best lawyer with the most influential law firm. The law is used by large powerful organizations to break the backs of other organizations and individuals that may have every right to put up opposition. Some influential institutions use the law as an offensive weapon to destroy their smaller competition. In some cases a suit can freeze the assets of a small company or individual and thus destroy them. Due the drawn out process of appeals, the high cost of cases, court fees, etc., many highly financed institutions enjoy virtual impunity. The law is friend to those with the means to purchase it.

Education

Money can be used to provide educational opportunity or to take opportunity away. It is amazing how the most critical of all institutions can ever be considered for budget reductions during tight economic times. Sometimes we are so unfeeling and stupid that we pick on those that are not in a position to defend themselves. Our children are a prime target. We also pick on the elderly and the homeless by cutting their financial support. We more directly shoot ourselves in the foot with regard to our children. We do not seem to realize that the future of the country and world is in their hands. We don't seem to understand that they are the ones that will take care of us in old age. In our selfish haste, it is evident that they will have a hefty burden placed on them in the future. Many young adults will have opportunity removed, and remain dependent on their parents, thus inhibiting the progress of this generation. Many policies such as social security have pit young against old in desperate political movements. The current generation of young adults feels betrayed by the selfish greed of the generations before them, and they realize that they will have to incur the cost.

Some efforts do exist for the improved education of our young folks. Often there's talk of improving schools and allowing parents the option of sending their kids to private school partially financed by the government. The "information highway" is seen as a mechanism to improve the education of our children. However, any good coming out of these activities is jeopardized by greedy, selfish adults that chose to further divide society. Based on access to these resources, they could be used as tools of division if the have nots keep having not, and the haves keep having access to the best facilities. No one truly profits in the larger picture. Restricting the education of others ultimately costs society money by producing human economic burdens.

Health

Our very medical well being is dependent on money. For those without insurance, there is limited care and no financial incentive for health care professionals to provide them with treatment. Those that are rich and have insurance, can afford the best hospitals, specialists, care, and treatment that money can buy. The health care industry should not be treated as a business. Hospitals should not be out to make a profit. Doctors should also not be out for profit by prescribing unnecessary treatment, referring people to their own clinics, and taking kickbacks from the drug industry. Doctors and hospitals need incentives to provide good care and should not be burdened with outrageous malpractice insurance. The health care industry must come to a meeting of the minds to provide equal quality of service to all citizens. A price cannot be put on life.

Two Sides of a Coin

Money can serve the purposes that we allow it to serve. If we have selfish motives, money can be used to promote these motives. If we have misplaced values and priorities, money can be funneled into those avenues. However, if our priorities and values shift from self indulgence, money may provide a vehicle of exchange and mutual benefit. I asked some friends a question when we took a trip to New York City, the purest bastion of capitalism. I said, "If given a choice between receiving a million dollars, or creating and instant world-wide environment of fairness and equality, which would you choose?" Of course it was a loaded question and I felt that there was only one answer. Surprisingly, both of my friends chose to take the million dollars. I was somewhat upset at what I considered to be a selfish response. I said to them that only the latter choice is viable, because in an environment of equality and justice, a truly talented individual would become a millionaire anyway. This is coupled by the satisfaction derived from opening the doors of opportunity for everyone. If we would radically reshift our selfish concerns, an environment of opportunity could be provided for all to benefit mutually.

Tool of the Disenfranchised

Many groups have elevated their down trodden condition by focusing on their economic base. These peoples' efforts have afforded them a secure lifestyle and empowered them with significant influence to provide for their future. These people have also provided themselves with the freedom to act on their own behalf without concern for offending those that may provide for their well being. They are self sufficient. They own their own businesses, schools, banks, and in some instances, countries. These groups have exploited the economic environment to provide themselves with freedom. Money can be used as an economic equalizer that causes some people to set aside their motives and loyalties for personal gain and greed. Focused groups of individuals can use these opportunistic people, who may actually disagree with the aims of those they work for, but defer their opinions for greed. Personally, I believe this is the answer. When each faction of America's citizenry is economically empowered and earns the respect of all others, we will have an environment of true opportunity and equality.

EON

Dividends of the Environment

The peace dividend of the disappearance of the cold war must be channeled into institutions in need of desperate assistance. Cleaning up the environment, education, shelter for the homeless, new highways, libraries, museums, medical research, farm subsidies, space exploration, and youth recreational activities could all be funded by the annual defense budget. We need to reallocate our resources as our changing world environment is shifting its focus. Interestingly enough, America has dropped sanctions in South Africa, signed NAFTA, and opened trade relations with Vietnam and China. Are these policies designed to provide opportunity or promote a system of international economic bondage to the advantage of the richest 2%? Time and human nature will tell.

A Narrow Perspective

It is the nature of this country to reward only immediate success. There is no award for second place. To much emphasis is put on winning and building a large pile of money in order to be considered successful. This country is result oriented. The substance of achievement is too often ignored and overshadowed by material reward. The lessons learned through hard work are often lost when a large monetary reward does not result from our efforts. Our focus on end results can often be a dangerous and life threatening practice. Often times we don't stop to think of the repercussions of our actions because we have been blinded by greed or some big pay off. We have little concern for the ill effects that result from the methods we choose. It doesn't matter that we may be doing harm to ourselves or to others, so long as the job is finished and we are rewarded. This shortsightedness is a serious problem for Americans and America. Planning for the future cannot be accomplished over night. Other countries such as Japan, plan 15 to 20 years ahead and have long lasting relationships and agreements between their institutions. Their strategic planning and long-term relationships, maintained even through hardship, give them a competitive advantage. America's fallout from shortsightedness has resulted in pollution, urban decay, prison growth, drugs, gangs, war, nuclear waste, and any other modern American problem that can be named. After our shortsightedness has caused a problem, we then naturally think of a quick fix solution. The solution leads to more problems because we merely treat the symptoms, not the cause. It's a vicious cycle that need be broken.

What America Must Do

America must simply become a broader, all-encompassing, non-selfish nation. This will require white males, who I seem to continue to reference, to re-educate themselves. It will require them to set aside their insecure egos, control obsession, judgmental & quick to dismiss attitude, and self-centered agendas. These creatures will either reeducate themselves or they will eventually be totally excluded and ostracized. Currently they are frightened because they see the environment changing. There is increased immigration, new rules on sexual harassment, minority hiring and set aside programs, and females continually making advances. The secure white male will not be harmed from the changing environment. However, those who are backing themselves into a corner based on paranoia, will have great deal of difficulty. White males are in a position to contribute to the growth and success of America if they so chose, or they can continue to restrict and inhibit its progress. I would never place the blame for all of Americas problems, past and present, on white males. That would give them to much credit. They are not that smart or powerful.

EON

However, I do feel that they are a key contributor to our current state of affairs. Due to the environment that white males chose to create for themselves, they have enacted exclusion as standard operating procedure. If you do not fit a white male mold, you are not eligible for mainstream employment. This is why the major export of this country is university degrees. An atmosphere of inclusion does not exist. In today's global environment America cannot afford this elitist attitude to continue and expect to survive world-wide competition. America must realize that oppression is not profitable. Pushing people into jail and other dead-end environments cannot continue. Those that need help must receive help. Don't jail junkies who usually do harm only to themselves, treat them for their illness. Don't cut welfare recipients off without an alternative to provide for themselves. Whites must decide if they desire to tear the walls down that they have built around themselves, the same walls that restrict this country's achievement. We speak of legalizing drugs and removing the monopoly. We must legalize education and break up that monopoly. No great mind can go to waste even if it belongs to someone who is not a child of privilege. This country will have to solve all of its waste problems in the environment and especially the continued waste of human resources.

Groups that are typically considered disadvantaged should not wait for all these wonderful things to happen to America. So called "minorities" and females should not wait for white males to realize the errors of their ways. Aside from the fact that we may all be waiting well into old age, we should assume a proactive stance and act on our own behalf to improve our condition. Each group must take their future and fate into their own hands. For black folks, I do not call for a push toward wide scale integration. I believe that this practice has weakened our institutions. I believe that we should coordinate with other groups in business relationships that are mutually beneficial. I believe that we should coordinate with other groups to develop an environment of mutual respect that gives everyone and opportunity to compete on equal ground. Certain

160

parties fear a level playing field because they realize that they lack natural ability. Without providing themselves advantage and placing others at a disadvantage, they have no chance at competing. They fully recognize the potential of the people that they selectively place at disadvantage. They need to get over it. America needs to stop running from itself because there is nowhere to go.

The role of government should be to provide for the well being of the nation and ALL its many diverse people. It should not impose itself in the personal lives of individuals or groups, but it should see to the existence of an environment of security and equality. Government must not continue to see to the well being of just a few influential well-financed groups. Those that work within the government should not be there working for selfish motives and the acquisition of power. Of chief importance is the office of the President. The attitudes of the leader of any organization are those that permeate the organization and trickle down to provide the foundation for its operation and policies. Those that work under the president will share his attitude toward leadership. It is of paramount importance that our executive official is a broad minded person concerned only with the well being of the country regardless of cost, belief, and personal interest.

On Newjack

What is a Newjack? Newjacks define themselves by their attitude, actions, image, unmitigated gaul, and leadership. We are the generation that chooses to accept the burden of vision, courage, family, community, strength, daring, assertiveness, and "make no excuse,""take no prisoner" entrepreneurship. We are the beneficiaries of the strides of our immediate and long gone forbearers. We have at this time everything that it takes to make a profound and shocking impact on the fabric of society. We are the new architects of our race, molding that which we will, into concrete reality. We arm ourselves with knowledge and faith that we can reclaim what is ours. We have no words or concern for those that impede our progress toward a destiny ordained by God. We also only love those that love us back, and do not have a "turn the other cheek" policy. We have prepared ourselves to deal in the post cold war era of covert racism by developing our awareness of self, and sensitizing ourselves to societies' signals. As Newjacks, we accept the responsibility of knowledge and do not duck our heads into the sand as events unfold. We take a stand, one way or the other. We are not fence straddlers. We have an underlying curiosity as to why and how this world works, and feed off of its energy. We are an optimistic group that sees failure and setback as a classroom and precursor to excellence and success. Every happening that we witness and experience enhances our development.

Where We Come From

Newjacks come from various backgrounds. Some from an impoverished humble existence, others children of privilege. Whatever the case may be, we at this juncture in our lives are thankful to those that came before us. Our family members and ancestors that are our reason for being. It is on their shoulders that we currently stand. In many instances, they sacrificed their character, dignity, history, names, and very lives to provide succeeding generations with a better way of life. Many died in the quest to free themselves from bondage. Many died as a result of refusing to be treated as less than men and women. Many died as a result of obtaining the right to vote. They could not possibly have dreamed of the opportunities that are available today as a result of their hundreds of years of sacrifice. Unfortunately, as a collective body we are gravely disappointing our predecessors with our lack of continued progress. Newjacks will be ever mindful of our duty to continue the work of those that came before us that sacrificed so much. Currently the pyramid of accomplishment that is being built by our people is only half finished. At this current rate of growth it will never reach an apex of ultimate achievement for our people. We Newjacks are those who will continue to build upon the foundation that has been laid by our forbearers. We are courageous enough to assume the risks and responsibility necessary for the continued advancement of our people. We will never become consumed with a comfortable lifestyle lacking of substance designed to assimilate into a mindless phony mainstream. This would require forgetting our history and our plans for shaping the future. This is unacceptable, and we do not give it a second thought. No sell out.

Our Responsibility

As time has passed it has become necessary to employ new tools and methods for the construction of the future. The ever-changing environment and urgency to rebuild our community at this time calls for aggressive tactics and bold methods. We Newjacks have the ability to employ these measures without being reckless yet not fearing the repercussions of the associated risk. We appreciate the methods of the past used by our leaders, however this is a new time and we cannot be bound by what may have worked to some extent in the past. We must throw away many of yesterdays' tactics, but not their principle. Today we exist in the world of technology. Due to certain advancements in computer science, we can command amazing power from the top of a desk. Every Newjack is intimately associated with today's fast paced world of technology. The future will be a determined by the development and utilization of software and communications. They are the tools to implement dreams of vision. Know them well.

We cannot count on others to show us the way to wealth, prosperity, and freedom. Most people will attempt to steer you off course because of jealousy, frustration, or fear that you may be successful and elevate your condition. Those who are secure in themselves and have your best interests at heart, are valuable assets. Newjacks are attuned to themselves and know their limitations. Therefore, they seek appropriate council to supplement their skills in order to achieve a greater good and end result.

Newjacks are self sufficient, yet not too proud or stupid to turn down help and guidance especially if there is an opportunity that has availed itself. That handkerchief head crap about pulling yourself up by your bootstraps is garbage. Everyone has had a break at some point in time. We cannot let pride stand in the way of progress. By that same token, we must be careful whom we align ourselves with. Those with the sincerest of intentions will not ask for deferred gain or favors.

Every Newjack is driven by a sense of fate. We must follow our respective paths with a sense of courage and fearlessness to see what the end will bring. We are not engaged in a popularity contest. They may hate us, they may curse us, but they will respect us. We have made a vow to destiny to ride the unpredictable currents back to the motherland regardless of outcome. We do not fear the repercussions of our actions because we are on the side of righteousness. The emotion of fear only elevates our energy level and heightens our awareness. It never stops us.

Newjacks are not obsessed with creating institutions that lack substance and provide a false sense of accomplishment. We are not chasing the European/American lifestyle of the privileged. Comforts have their place, in that we must feel physically secure and have a true refuge of solitude and acceptance that we call home. However, being on the A-list, driving and drinking the latest, and acting like soulless devils that measure each other by bank account is not nation building. It is ultimately destructive because we chase the aspects of the material world that will in turn once again enslave us.

Newjacks must use their individual talents and career skills to build the future. We are not obsessed with making all the right moves to climb the corporate ladder. We are again entrepreneurs, learning all that we can to build a future for our community. The price of working for someone else for to long is far too costly. We are required to modify our behavior in order to assimilate. We end up distancing ourselves from our community and stirring all sorts of internal conflicts that can be avoided. Corporate America can be an education that can ultimately be put to use if you don't stay long enough to have 2.5 kids, a mortgage, a BMW and few options. At this point it becomes a difficult trap to escape.

A Newjack is anchored by his or her family. This strong family unit provides the support for our dynamic activity. It is the separate world that we seek sanctuary from fierce battle. We recharge ourselves through our families. Our families provide the key link to perpetuating a future rich with possibilities. We cherish our families and safeguard their well being with our very lives. Those that chose to violate the sanctity of a Newjacks family, are prepared to die as a result of their action.

The Environment

Today, we are forced to navigate a world filled with diversion, temptation, and traps. The reason so many people are confused and see no future is because the environment in which we live is so volatile and dynamic. The players don't wear numbers and there is no program that lists the members of the opposing team. Only a Newjack armed with self awareness and fortitude will survive and thrive. The option to not participate in society is made overwhelmingly available through the use of material escapism's, drugs, alcohol, assimilation, and self destruction. Many would choose this route and many others are willing to lead you down its dead end path. For a Newjack, consideration of this avenue of cowardice is synonymous with suicide.

This world is a ball of confusion comprised of opposing forces in constant flux. Forces shift, reshift, settle, and then shift again. Today we can no longer be solely concerned with domestic issues. Technology and communications have shrunk our world into one global community and economy. This is not to say that we will all one day live as one, side by side. The larger community will be composed of smaller, cohesive, discrete communities. These separate communities will be concerned with their individual advancement and survival. They will form alliances with other groups when there are mutual advantages. Groups that bring nothing to the table, groups that are not cohesive and bound by mutual respect, groups that do not have an agenda or idea of their role in the larger community, groups that do not have the ability to provide, sustain, and defend themselves, will simply be dissipated, disenfranchised, and destroyed. No single individual will become successful without the support of their community and family. Any such individual without this type of support will be forced to align himself with a foreign community that does not have their interests at heart. This individual will be forced to support the agenda of the group that funds him even if it means the harm or destruction of the disenfranchised community to which he is naturally a member.

Seeking equality and parity with other communities will not be the aim of the future. Parity with those who are dissimilar to us, or who have oppressed us is far to low a goal to set for ourselves. Communities will establish respect by determining what is best for themselves and achieving it. To seek becoming similar in culture to another group is to state that what you are has no value. It is to state that you have nothing special or unique to contribute to this world. You bring nothing to the table. It states that you have given up on the development of self because you have determined that your potential also has no value. It is the ultimate surrender of cowardice. Imitation is only the sincerest form of flattery when you make conscious effort to honor someone. It is also the fallback for those that have no talent nor the ability to recognize what makes them special.

So how do Newjacks fight through the confusion without compromising ourselves or making excuses to fail? We fight by attuning ourselves to the environment and staying ever aware of what transpires around us. We steer clear or eliminate forces that intend to do us harm or impede our progress. We have no tolerance for those who desire to implement their agendas and programs at our expense. The key to our ability to continue fighting is linked to a stable social atmosphere that provides support and sees to our basic needs. An individual that is distracted by a daily quest for food, shelter, clothing, purpose, and social acceptance is not able to take offensive action to implement change and shape the future. If you look at the condition of the black community this will be apparent. We must see to the stability of our social support base and provide ourselves a place of uncompromised acceptance.

Along with the stability of our social infrastructure, we must continue to develop our sense of self awareness. We must become in tune with the history of our people. We must become in tune with ourselves in order to recognize what special gift and contribution each of us has. We must recognize our weakness and work to eliminate them as well as solicit help when necessary. When we empower ourselves with self awareness, our destinies will begin to unfold. We will become masters of our souls. The desire to assimilate and migrate toward the mainstream will altogether disappear. The ability of others to persuade us to assist them in implementing their agenda will cease. Only when you reach a state of self awareness is it possible to recognize activities that are designed to improve your condition or do you harm. Becoming self aware is like sitting in the captain's chair of a seaworthy craft steering clear of bad weather and obstacles, sailing an ocean of destiny.

As Newjacks, we are fully aware of the cyclic nature of existence. We know that our time will indeed come. We need simply to prepare ourselves and recognize the opportunity. Luck is when preparation meets opportunity. The world is shifting faster and the ability to recognize that opportunity grows increasingly challenging. However, powerful tools have been developed for informed individuals to keep pace. The talk of information coming from all directions on a digital highway into the home may seem intimidating. For a Newjack, this spells opportunity. This opportunity can only be taken advantage of if we supplement our access to information with the ability to recognize which information is of importance. Even then, the information has no meaning if we do not act upon it with decisive intent. The possibilities of the future and the opportunities that will avail themselves give us purpose. Even with the adversity faced today, the current challenges, the setbacks, and the ongoing struggle for survival, a Newjack still finds these exciting times to live in. At this instant in time, everything is possible.

Attitude

It is safe to say that Newjacks have "Attitude." Some may mistake it for arrogance. That's their problem. Some will be intimidated. That's their insecurity. Some will be jealous. They have no faith in their abilities. Regardless of people's opinion, a Newjack remains unswayed. We are also tolerant of ignorance, and refuse to accept a burden of educating those that do not truly seek the light of knowledge. This would be an exhaustive job. Not to say that we will turn our backs on people, but we don't cast our pearls amongst swine either. We also need not expose ourselves to the frustration of attempting to educate those that have no true intent to share our vision. We must focus on the activities and practices that build a future, as well as those who have a sincere desire to take part in building a nation. With that, I depart by leaving you with a few Newjackisims in no particular order of importance. Peace. I'll be back.

Newjackisims

Most people don't even take time to ask why they believe what they believe. If it has been indoctrinated or is tradition, that's good enough. Newjacks question everything fearlessly.

EON

A Newjack realizes that he/she cannot save everyone or do everything. The best leaders have the best support from others that share their vision.

◆

A major step in becoming a Newjack is to develop your own ideology to live life.

◆

Systems are designed to be manipulated by those with the correct information. Those who are not informed will be manipulated by the system.

◆

We prefer to work 18 hours a day living our dreams as opposed to working 8 to fulfill someone else's.

◆

Newjacks are so in touch with their history that each has lived and died a thousand times. We are the accumulation of our past.

◆

Newjacks don't wait for a leader or savior. We step forward.

◆

Our elders have much to offer. Honor them and listen to them.

◆

Realize that your money, your job, car, house can all be taken away on any given day. You can be stripped of everything. Take time to empower yourself with knowledge and skills to rebuild should this happen.

◆

Newjacks must make a spiritual connection. The loneliness of an empty soul will drive you crazy.

◆

Newjacks realize that there is a time to offend and upset the illusion of balance. Newjacks know when to do so, and do so without hesitation. Timing and coordination are critical elements to the initiation of any revolution.

Newjack means that you make the statement to white people that: "I am the manifestation of your greatest fear. Black, young, educated, focused, undaunted. Burn your cross in my yard. It will be a pleasure to work by the light given off by its glow. The light will also illuminate you for my cross hairs.

◆

Newjacks salute the entrepreneurship of those ethnic groups in America that are thriving. We will learn how they achieved success, and do better.

◆

Newjacks, your worst fear should be not fulfilling your destiny. Your nightmare should be to look back and say, "I should have, I could have." Don't look back in 20-30 years and discover that you took no part in your people's advancement.

◆

Salute the ideas and spirit of integration, the pioneers that risked everything for what they believed in the go to school, get a degree, get a job mentality. Newjacks, we must refocus our efforts since integration is not the answer.

◆

Newjacks, visualize your goals, quantify them specifically, write them down, internalize them, achieve them.

◆

Newjacks, time is more valuable than money. If you lose a dollar and you're smart enough, you can make back two dollars. The unforgiving second is gone forever.

◆

The only revenge is success.

◆

Our ancestors scream from their graves for our achievement. Don't dishonor those ole Africans.

◆

We are confronted with the challenge of putting back together the fragmented puzzle of our communities.

EON

Those of us that love life, celebrate it through risk.

◆

Newjacks, we sit at the cross roads between civil rights and pure entrepreneurship. Take the ball and run.

◆

Money brings independence, freedom, and power, not happiness.

◆

Newjacks, regardless of whom you are working for, always be working for yourself. Have an agenda.

◆

In this life you will accomplish one million times as much if you develop the ability to work through people. Not use people like they are disposable, but be an entrepreneur and place them in an environment that allows them to work as they work best, and provide them with opportunity to develop themselves.

◆

Newjacks realize that we cannot change whites' attitudes by active dialog. We waste time. Nor should we assume the burden of their education. Action will speak all the words that need to be spoken. Economic, social, political action.

◆

Only through a high degree of success, fulfillment and achievement in your personal life can you genuinely celebrate the achievements of others.

◆

Newjacks, realize that your potential is limitless. However if you don't work hard to explore it you are doing yourself and your people a disservice.

◆

Newjacks must find a way to work together right now. We can talk out our differences as we stand together on the chest of our mutual oppressor.

◆

Newjacks, pressure elevates our game to the next level of competition.

Newjacks must come to know whom we work for. Often the benefactors of our work are buried in layers of documentation, job titles, and bureaucracy. We may discover that we are working against ourselves.

◆

Newjacks struggle to elevate our conscience and soul from the limited confines that the European value system America imposes.

◆

Do not develop a preconceived notion about any issue or individual. Evaluate the facts as they present themselves and then develop a position.

◆

Newjacks don't give a damn about being liked, loved, or hated. We desire only to be respected by denying people the ability to ignore us.

◆

We accept the burden of responsibility and knowledge willingly.

◆

We are not islands, nor do we work in a vacuum. Place a high value on your family and friends.

◆

Newjacks create jobs. Don't strive to be employed.

◆

Be careful of whom you share your dreams with. People become weary of independent thinkers and those that take initiative to improve their condition. They may hold you back. Seek out those that share your vision.

◆

Don't allow yourself to be validated or invalidated by someone else's standards.

◆

Too many of us are going after happiness and comfort instead of greatness. The burden of a Newjack is the latter. If happiness comes with greatness so be it.

Don't get selfish and cast aside the sacrifices of those before you for that lame little 30K job and a condo. We have the responsibility to build. If you are like me, you may be the biggest gamble that your family has ever ventured upon. Take a chance at becoming and entrepreneur right now. You can always go back to that lame little job.

◆

Beware the signs of a Newjack. You begin to think differently. You begin to imagine a new reality. You begin to question your destiny and that of your people. You take charge of your destiny and define a new reality.

◆

Realize that there is a solution to every single problem. They have yet to invent the problem with no solution. The solution may be complex, but there is an answer. It may take a life's worth of commitment.

◆

It was said by one of our great leaders that "If blood must be shed, let it be our blood, not the blood of our enemies." Not to dishonor our hero who said this, but Newjacks love those that love us back.

◆

Newjacks assume activities that have value. Let those activities eleviate your burden in a constructive healthy manner. Stay in a constant state of education and learn from everyone.

◆

Newjacks, work a little each and every day on your dream. Even if for just 5 minutes.

◆

Newjacks, you do yourself a disservice by not fulfilling your destiny. Frustration and a feeling of powerlessness can be overcome only by action.

◆

Newjacks, let your actions be known when they reach a level of maturity. Granted, it is dangerous to make early plans public knowledge, but it is also dangerous to keep plans and actions secrete from those that share your vision. You can inspire as well as be inspired by those that share your dreams. Tap into this synergy. If you do not make your works known, a fate may befall you where you need support. Any would be leader moving alone is subject for destruction.

Newjacks, we allow no one to establish a timetable or schedule for our advancement.

Newjacks, don't waste the energy of your youth on meaningless pursuits. Realize the unforgiving nature of time, and how much of it we have each been allotted on this earth.

◆

We must again purchase our freedom through diligent work and sacrifice.

APPENDIX

20 Tactics of Oppression

Those that aim to control, influence, and oppress, employ certain tactics and strategies to pursue their goals. These tactics are aimed directly at us individually and at our community. Often times we fall prey to them due to lack of information that would allow us to develop countermeasures. I do not attempt to lay the claim that these tactics or those who use them are solely responsible for our condition. Again, that would give them far to much credit and power. The only way to remove the effectiveness of these tactics is to combat them from a standpoint of recognition and action. An adversary cannot use a tactic that is readily recognizable to further their causes. It is my intent to begin to analyze the offensive strategies used against us for various purposes. What I suggest are but a few observations not a finite all encompassing list. When we begin to think and analyze occurrences, situations, and statements from the proper perspective and point of view, we will enable ourselves to recognize what is intended to do us harm regardless of the way it presents itself. We need not develop a finite all encompassing list. We must develop a method of thinking that will enable us to analyze situations and take action.

Tactic 1: Divide and Conquer

One of the most basic and time tested tactics of oppression is that of division. A divided, uncoordinated people are unable to implement change and cannot resist those that desire to impose change against their will. The most effective form of division is to cause dissension in the ranks of an adversary. If a fighting force can be made preoccupied by internal struggle, they become weak and ineffective. Whites have always attempted to promote division in the black community from the days of slavery when light skinned slaves were allowed to work in the house, while the darker slaves were left in the field. Natural jealousy and elitism arose between lighter skinned blacks and darker skinned blacks. This is still prevalent in our community today as we still value lighter skin and "good hair" as opposed to African features. Whites encourage this division by allowing those that accept conformity certain advantages over those that do not conform. Those that change their language, demeanor, and sometimes physical appearance to more closely mimic that of whites are given certain concessions. Those of our own that speak out against our culture and deny where they came from are also given preferential treatment and a great deal of air play and exposure in order to encourage their behavior.

Whites encourage the division of our people so that they can more effectively manage our threat and the potential that we possess. If black people are ever put back in touch with ourselves and our history it will mean the end of white authority. Whites fully know that it would be impossible to control an organized black people with an agenda. Therefore, they instinctively attempt to retard the development of our power base. If we look at the continent of Africa as an example, we can see the Europeans descended on the mother land and carved it up like a dinner foul. They disenfranchised and enslaved our people and erected boarders to segment the land. In the process they killed millions. In effect they attempted to destroy our foundation by destroying our home land and disconnecting us from our origins. They did not count on the fact the our spirit bonds us, transcends physical distance, and cannot be destroyed.

On of the most obvious areas that is targeted for division is between the black male and the black female. If this bond is effectively breached, we lose our method of procreation and our race effectively dies. The attempts to split us along lines of gender is evident in the white master taking our women and bastardizing our children. Black men are also stigmatized to be monsters that are incapable of responsibility and heading households. Many of our own women speak the worst of our black men due to bad experiences with immature men and men that have abandoned their families. Our men are raised by single parent female households where boys are not shown how to become men by following the example of men. Welfare is a systematic way of economically driving men out of the house and disenfranchising our community. In the work force, black women are making strides that exceed those of black males. This is due to the fact that we have some thorough sistas that are simply doing it, and by the fact that white males want to devalue the existence of black men. White men will always have a fascination with black women, and will attempt to drive a wedge between black men and women to dissuade us from taking our rightful places next to one another. The black women will usually be approached by white men with incentives to distance themselves from us. We cannot betray one another and expect to survive in order to reclaim our thrones.

Whites saw the opportunity that integration presented and seized it with vigor. They fully recognized our desire to enter white institutions to prove ourselves and be accepted on white terms. They realized that the weakening of our own institutions would occur and we would self destruct. To this day, our communities are weakened by our most talented people working for large white firms indoctrinated into a system of soulless bottom line values. These values permeate our community and we lose touch. We move out of our neighborhoods in body and in spirit.

Tactic 2: Feed the Denial

Whites must feed their sense of denial continually in order to perpetuate their actions. Whites must continually make issue of those of us who are seemingly successful. They attempt to bring this small percentage to the forefront as though our successful minority is common place. They parade those of us who have a little money in order to say "hey look at this guy, he made it, these people have no excuse and I should not feel guilt regardless of what I do or what took place in the past." The salaries and money of our successful minority are the first to be mentioned in the public spotlight in accords with this tactic.

White denial often forces them to paint them selves as part of the natural landscape. Whites in black countries such as Jamaica and South Africa actually believe that they are members of the indigenous people. Many whites call themselves Africans. This complete blind ignorance is an attempt to downplay and totally ignore the history of conquest and murder of the whites that inhabit black countries as residents and decedents of those that spilled black blood. The decedents of settlers that had no right to be there to begin with.

White denial is of course the method by which they detach themselves from reality and the evil that they have done and currently do. It allows them to justify the continuation of their selfish actions without regard for the feelings and rights of others. Whites simply deny the right of nonwhite people to govern themselves and be respected as all humans should be.

Tactic 3: Erase Our History

To this day we have no shortage of attempts to suppress our full story and deny the truth about our history. This continued war against our past is waged so that we devalue ourselves and society devalues us. All people that successfully navigate this world we exist in have a strong sense of their history. It is human nature to derive a sense of purpose and belonging from knowledge of our origins. If this tie to the past is broken, it is like disabling the foundation of a building. Eventually the entire structure will crumble. The desire is to keep us out of touch with ourselves and disconnected from our rich legacy of the past. If we had knowledge of ourselves and became self aware, no one could impose their will against us. The insecure that have made oppression their purpose in life would live in fear at the existence of a united, self aware, black, race. Many would find themselves and their illusion of superiority totally destroyed by truth. Therefore, it is necessary to continue efforts aimed at destroying our self concept so that the inflated self concept of those that attempt to oppress us can be maintained.

Tactic 4: Imply Superiority

Whites practice a very sophisticated form of racism. It deals with the attempt to implant images of inferiority into the subconscious while implanting images of white superiority. Negative imagery is all around us in many diverse forms. Whites have found it much simpler to bombard the mind with messages of inferiority and the implied superiority of white people. Campaigns waged against our leaders and against those that we hold high in our community are aimed to send a signal that we will never reach a level of parity regardless of our accomplishments. Modern day white male criminals receive no punishment and are rewarded with book deals and movies for committing crimes costing billions of dollars. This implies that they are untouchable and above the judgment of others. The physical beating of Rodney King was intended to reinforce the fact that black lives have no value. The acquittal of the white male overseers, I mean officers, demonstrated that white males are above the law.

Tactic 5: Attempt to Define and Acceptable Profile for Society

Whites carve out their niche by defining where they would like to place the members of nonwhite society. There must be people to join the military, people to dig ditches, people to clean up after whites, people to fill the jails, and so on. By whites constricting the development of certain people, they channel them into the roles that they would have them play. There are methods of measurement that gather demographic data such as the census so that trends can be traced and acted upon. Redistricting and political as well as economic disenfranchisement are tools of the trade. Once they have defined a niche or market for themselves they must effectively keep others out. When they find an area that they want to assume control over, it is done as quietly and gradually over as much time as possible. Other more obvious tactics are used which murder and displace people. Colonization still exists to this day where the European powers have considerable interests over seas. The colonization and total rape of Africa were done at the expense of Africans to the advantage of Europeans.

Tactic 6: Offer False Opportunity

Whites will offer false opportunity in order to appease and discourage. After we have come begging at their door enough times, whites will eventually offer us a bone to shut us up. This false opportunity provides us with an artificial sense of arrival and achievement. Usually what we are offered is of little value and we end up serving the interests of those that employ us. We will never be placed into a position that truly enables us to influence our own destiny. Those opportunities are made for self, not given.

Often in the work place, whites give false opportunity with the intention of discrediting us. At times they will throw so much at us that success becomes an impossible task within a reasonable period of time. They offer no support, encouragement, or guidance. Our orchestrated failure leads to our own self doubt and unavoidable dismissal from the job. It also feeds the denial of whites were they can say that "we did give them a chance." Many false opportunities are intended to provide a vehicle to stigmatize, calling us "affirmative action baby" and as a result we become invalidated regardless of our accomplishments. We will see how these new "diversity" programs in the work place truly play out. Most whites at large "elite" corporations and universities feel that no black could truly earn a right to be there based on individual merit. Whites will make excuses for their shortcomings by stating that an affirmative action recipient or quota was the cause of their lack of advancement.

Tactic 7: Create Negative Imagery to Demonize

This tactic attempts to dehumanize us so that the conclusion is reached that we are unworthy of respect. It is intended to make people believe that we are worthy of being treated in any manner in which people feel appropriate. This was the primary tactic used in the Rodney King trial that made light of his past police record so that people felt that he was deserving of his beating. Black people are made out to be the primary recipients of welfare, the primary users of drugs, the most violent members of society, and the representatives for the lowest tier of society. There are attempts to define our entire race by our downtrodden minority members. We are often treated like an infectious disease that will take over America, if America does not take actions to control and subjugate us.

Tactic 8: Inflict a Collective Culpability Complex

Whites attempt to make it seem that each of us is responsible in some way for the collective of black behavior. If one makes a statement in the media or takes some action, we are all expected to comment, atone, apologize, discredit, or disassociate ourselves from the individual or group making the statement. We are expected to explain for one another. This tactic is used against us to inflict a collective guilt complex on our people. This tactic supplements their goal of division where they attempt to foster dissent by making our weaker brothers and sisters explain to the even weaker brothers and sisters that "if anyone makes trouble, it will be made difficult for all of us, so just stay in line." The worst we can ever do is apologize or explain away the actions of one of our own.

Tactic 9: Discredit any Institution Geared at Improving our Condition

Often whites will attempt to discredit institutions and ideas that are geared specifically at improving the condition of our people. They are so selfish that they see no need for an NAACP, minority set asides, affirmative action, or historically black universities and colleges. In their ignorance they assume that this is bias and provides us with unfair advantage. They will attempt to state that there is no national association for the advancement of white people, no historically white universities and colleges. To them I say, "Why would you need any institution such as this when you have an entire country that is built around catering to your needs already." They have Congress, the Federal Reserve and *the board rooms of every single fortune 500 corporation in America*! Yet they have the gaul and arrogance to bitch about the measures that I have to take to correct the discrimination, ignorance and bias they have imposed. The sheer nerve!

Tactic 10: Utilize Diversion to Get Some Wiggle Room

Often times whites will take the light and focus off of a sensitive issue by diverting attention elsewhere. In order to divert maximum attention almost instantaneously, whites will use blacks as a scapegoat. If a white person commits a crime, naming a black suspect diverts maximum attention. This has been done on numerous occasions. Diverting attention is also used for political and financial scandal. Often times wars have been waged to divert the country's attention away from domestic issues and the political fallout that would result. This was attempted during the Gulf War, however our victorious war time president was unable to secure another term in office because the issues that he wanted to downplay with his "line in the sand" turned out to be to pressing. Whites will always promote a certain degree of disorder in society so that their actions can go unnoticed. When the rest of us are caught up in the struggle for survival battling conditions imposed to consume our energy and attention, we cannot take the time to question the sophisticated divisive policies of this county.

Tactic 11: Get Someone Else to do the Fighting

Whites have always practiced the brilliantly wicked strategy of getting lackeys and puppets to fight their battles for them. Whites prefer to remain isolated from the actual evil that they perpetrate and the consequences of their actions. Their sense of denial makes them seek alternative measures to implement their agendas without physically getting blood on their hands. This tactic also provides them with the option of placing culpability with those that they swindled into fighting for them.

Tactic 12: Assume Partial Credit for Correcting White Injustices

Whites never want to look *all* bad. After they are compelled to acknowledge their past transgressions due to our efforts to humanize them, they attempt to stand side by side with us as though they took part in the corrective action. When their weak attempts at resisting change and justice fail, they attempt to flip the script and take part in the credit for changing their racist policies. They will often times promote some white male that has always been a "champion of civil rights" so that one of their own is visible on the winning team. Whites never want to be totally caught on the losing side of any issue. They must play a role in every big victory. Their collective mind set may be on one side, but not their political physical bodies.

Tactic 13: Discredit the Efforts Geared Toward Self Enlightenment

Whites feel the threat of the emerging self awareness of blacks on the horizon. They have seen this trend before in the 60s and 70s and realize its potential if it ever truly takes root. Whites attempt to discredit Afrocentric studies. They will state that more lies should not be used to cover up other older lies. They simply fear the truth, what it will reveal, and its repercussions.

Tactic 14: Throw People of Balance by Making Them Emote

Whites realize that they can throw us off balance by playing to our emotions. They know that we are a naturally expressive emotional people. Often times we will slip into and emotional tirade and lose grasp of reality and the purpose of our efforts. Whites will bait us into emotional responses, especially at work, so that they are justified in removing us from our positions. We will be called "unmanageable" or "a problem worker" since we do not maintain the phony face and posture that whites adopt in the work place. Whites realize that luring us into an emotional response effectively diffuses our ability to implement a rational plan of action.

Tactic 15: Desensitize Society

Whites attempt to raise our tolerance for their ignorance and criminal activity. The primary tool for this tactic is the effective manipulation of the media, from Hollywood to the local newspaper. White males continue to defraud the government via political action and under the table monetary transactions. It becomes commonplace and accepted that white crime cannot be prosecuted to the extent that black crime is prosecuted. Our acceptance of this double standard only leads to the continuation and perpetuation of this practice. Our inundation with untouchable white criminals that act with impunity makes us reassess our value as dictated by their standards that do not apply to us.

Tactic 16: Demonstrate Loyalty to the White Consciousness by Demonizing Black People

President Clinton utilized Sista Soulja in order to reassure his white male peers that he would not totally pander to the needs and concerns of black America. President Bush did the same thing with Willie Horton. Whites will cast an aspersion directed specifically at our race, which is intended to reassure the white collective of continued solidarity across the continuum. There was a time when whites would simply go and hang someone of our race in order to unite themselves. This practice is no longer as widely accepted, so they continue to demonstrate their loyalty to the collective by stigmatizing us in the media. Individuals like Senator Hollings who considers Africans starving savages implicitly sings the rallying call of his own people.

Tactic 17: Dress for the Emotional and Political Climate

The white consciousness is simply that of chameleon. Whatever the prevailing societal wind dictates is what whites publicly do. When they are interviewed as to whether they would vote for a black or support an issue benefiting our people, they adopt an attitude of liberal agreement. However, what they say and what they do in action are usually two altogether different things. They embrace the doctrines that support their wishes for today. They are short term thinkers concerned with immediate needs. It is similar to the way in which Rome adopted the tenants of Christianity after murdering and persecuting Christians and crucifying Christ. That which is denounced today may well be accepted tomorrow. They are the most duplicitous and divisive people that have ever existed. The direction they take depends which way the wind is blowing.

Tactic 18: Tie Up Our Resources by Having us Bare the Burden of Their Education

They have some of us dedicating our lives to fighting racism. They realize that they can tie up some or our resources by getting us to fight this battle. The more they perpetuate their ignorance, the more some of us are willing to pick up the torch to fight this futile battle. Our efforts are diverted from substantive activities that will lead to our advancement.

Tactic 19: You Should Be So Happy to Have This Good Fortune...Nigga

They will often place us in a position where we have to publicly state that we are so happy to be treated so well. They ask us to participate in their denial. They like to hear how happy we are. We falsely reassure that we are so happy to be working for them and that we feel that we are being treated fairly. Though we feel that we are being treated like crap, we dare not say so since we may lose our job or business. The white collective typically keeps some lackeys on hand that will make these reassuring public declarations. This is especially useful if there is a court case where they need to show how fair minded and liberal they treat us.

Tactic 20: Dilute our Talent Pool

If white organizations are going to have to put up with blacks, they want our best and most talented. They expect super niggas that walk on water. They rarely accommodate the opportunity to learn and make mistakes. This is why they target our most exceptional achievers. They make the bait very sweet by offering attractive salaries. They realize that we have paid a premium for our education and have mounted up thousands of dollars in loans. This of course depletes our own talent pool within our community. We usually take the bait when offered positions in white institutions since we have a natural tendency to integrate in order to validate our self worth. This has caused us much damage over the years and continues to deplete our talent pool. Half of our best work for the government invisible behind layers of bureaucracy. Wealth can only be built in the private sector.